Life-Serving Boundaries

6 Practical Skills for Creating Thriving Relationships

by Elia Paz

Life-Serving Boundaries
6 Practical Skills for Creating Thriving Relationships

by Elia Paz

Copyright © 2024 Wise Heart.
All rights reserved.
Published by Elia Paz / Wise Heart
ISBN 979-8-9998254-0-7

We offer our sincere gratitude to those who have directly contributed to this book including Jeri Parks, Jean McElhaney, and Rosa Ramirez.

And we offer deep gratitude for the many key teachers that made this work possible such as Marshall Rosenberg, Donna Roy, Jon Eisman, and Hogen Bays.

TABLE OF CONTENTS

INTRODUCTION 6
- The Traditional Understanding of Boundaries
- The Value of Life-Serving Boundaries
- The New Framework of Life-Serving Boundaries

OVERVIEW OF MINDFUL COMPASSIONATE DIALOGUE 16
- Nonviolent Communication
- Hakomi Body-Centered Therapy
- Mindfulness

LIFE-SERVING BOUNDARIES: SKILL 1 29
When saying "no" to someone's request, identify the needs to which you are saying "yes"
- Thriving
- Attuning to needs
- Equanimity with needs
- Stewardship of needs

LIFE-SERVING BOUNDARIES: SKILL 2 42
Identify 3 types of Life-Serving Boundaries
- Why is it helpful to divide boundaries regarding connection into three types?
- Setting a distant boundary
- Setting a flexible boundary
- Setting a close boundary

LIFE-SERVING BOUNDARIES: SKILL 3 58
Articulate 3 non-negotiable boundaries that you hold in any relationship
- What is a non-negotiable boundary?
- What does it take to know and set yours?

TABLE OF CONTENTS

LIFE-SERVING BOUNDARIES: SKILL 4 81
Identify current limiting beliefs that interfere with boundary setting and the expansive beliefs that will support boundary setting
- Limiting beliefs
- Expansive beliefs
- How to evaluate boundaries

LIFE-SERVING BOUNDARIES: SKILL 5 123
Identify the signs and symptoms of behavior in yourself or others that don't support boundaries
- Enmeshment, and disengagement
- Common behaviors that don't support Life-Serving Boundaries
- Subtle behaviors that don't support Life-Serving Boundaries

LIFE-SERVING BOUNDARIES: SKILL 6 151
Establish a boundary with body language, behavior, or words any time that you would like to change or disengage from an interaction
- Setting boundaries with reactivity
- Setting boundaries while repairing boundary violations

CONCLUSION 199

APPENDIX 204

INTRODUCTION

THE TRADITIONAL UNDERSTANDING OF BOUNDARIES

Traditional ideas of boundaries focus on what you don't want. Thus, setting a boundary is about closing off, pushing someone away, or expressing an angry "no" in the face of something unwanted. Such actions are often associated with being tough and may be accompanied by harsh judgments of yourself or others.

This traditional way of thinking about and enacting boundaries ignores what you do want in a given relationship or situation. It also bypasses opportunities to set boundaries in small instances in everyday life. When you lose track of what's important to you in small moments there is an additive effect in which you end up in relationships or situations that don't work for you. Disentangling yourself from a relationship dynamic or situation that has been ongoing can be painful and difficult for all parties involved.

THE VALUE OF SETTING LIFE-SERVING BOUNDARIES

Learning to set Life-Serving Boundaries is a Relationship Competency that helps you embody an authentic life and live respectfully with others.

Setting Life-Serving Boundaries is a practice in which you discern and direct energy toward what you do want. When you make decisions based on your heartfelt values, most of the time you will naturally exclude what you don't want. Life-Serving Boundaries help you stay clear, stable, and focused on what truly serves life. They help you thrive and contribute to the well-being of others in a sustainable and meaningful way.

When you trust yourself to set Life-Serving Boundaries, you become less vulnerable to reactivity. You have a sense of confidence that you can meet challenges and stay true to your deepest values. This allows you to stay heart-connected, and consistently access wisdom and offer loving-kindness to yourself and others.

When boundaries are unclear, hyper-flexible, or ridgid, a sense of threat can invade your relationships and destabilize your ability to expand and grow.

However, when boundaries are clear and consistent in any relationship or partnership, or even between you and yourself, you can relax into a confidence that you can handle life's challenges.

Having clarity about Life-Serving Boundaries in relationships enhances a sense of security and freedom. When you are clear about boundaries for yourself and others, you also know where you are free to play and grow together.

THE NEW FRAMEWORK OF LIFE-SERVING BOUNDARIES

Life-Serving Boundaries are about honoring authenticity and what really works best in a given situation. Setting Life-Serving Boundaries means having clarity about what really meets needs or is in accord with core values, and then making a conscious decision about how to relate to another or behave in a particular situation while being able to remain heart-connected.

WHEN YOU TRUST YOURSELF TO SET LIFE-SERVING BOUNDARIES YOU BECOME LESS VULNERABLE TO REACTIVITY

Life-Serving Boundaries are about discerning what kind of behavior and decisions will best meet the needs in a given situation. Rather than a simple yes or no, this involves a subtle and complex discernment process either inwardly or in collaboration with others. Most importantly, setting Life-Serving Boundaries requires you to stay self-connected—that is, connected to the needs and values up for you in the moment. It is about standing in a clear "yes" with regard to what matters most.

Life-Serving Boundaries call us to cultivate and engage a subtle and refined sense of how to stand firm in what we care about, while remaining connected to a sense of respect and consideration for others.

Rather than deciding what you should or shouldn't do, learning to set Life-Serving Boundaries is based on discernment about what serves life. This discernment comes from being deeply grounded in universal needs and values like fairness, inclusion, respect, love, care, and community—to name a few. It's about learning what truly supports thriving.

To set Life-Serving Boundaries, you need to be able to recognize and honor your own needs, speak clearly about them, understand the verbal and behavioral language of boundary setting, honor the needs of others without taking responsibility for them, and engage in healing work with regard to your experiences of boundary violations in the past.

This also means learning about and understanding relationship dynamics—those that serve life and those that don't. Damaging relationship dynamics escalate when there is a lack of boundaries. These relationship dynamics include enmeshment, codependency, domestic violence, "power over," "power under," one-sided caretaking, etc.

In concrete terms, setting a Life-Serving Boundary means making a conscious decision about how you will relate to another, or behave in a particular situation. This means having clarity about what meets your needs and what doesn't relative to:

- The level of connection you have with another
- The environment you are in
- Types of engagement or activities
- Ways of relating to others

Such clarity allows you to put your attention and resources where you want them to go. Discerning and setting Life-Serving Boundaries rests on the empowering belief that you can find a way to honor your own needs in harmony with others.

> **YOU CAN FIND A WAY TO HONOR YOUR OWN NEEDS IN HARMONY WITH OTHERS**

BEING ABLE TO SET LIFE-SERVING BOUNDARIES CONSISTENTLY ARISES FROM THE INTEGRATION OF THE FOLLOWING:

1. Honor and self-responsibility with regards to your needs

2. Respect and care for the needs of others, while remaining grounded in your choice

3. The capacity to express what you are willing or not willing to do in concrete, specific, and doable terms

Let's look at how these three things play out in an example. Imagine you're negotiating boundaries with your mom. It's a Friday evening and you have just arrived home from work. You receive a call from your mother. She asks you to come over tomorrow, and spend the afternoon helping her with a project. Feelings of dread and tension begin to fill you. Feelings alert us to what matters to us—our needs (see the appendix for a list of universal needs). Wanting to honor your feelings and take responsibility for them, you realize you want to identify what matters to you in this situation.

"Mom," you say, "Let me call you back. I need to unwind from work before making plans for tomorrow. I will call you back and let you know before the end of the night."

You can set a boundary by deciding not to answer the question immediately. After you unwind and eat dinner, you continue to reflect on the situation. You first identify your thoughts, feelings, and needs. You also consider other aspects of the situation. Your mother is terminally ill. Your thoughts about how you think you should behave with her trigger guilt. You remind yourself that you don't want to connect with your mom simply out of guilt, or a sense of obligation. So you ask yourself what's keeping you from easily saying "yes" to her request? In other words, what needs are you wanting to take care of or meet instead of contribution?

The more you reflect, the more you begin to honor your own needs. You have worked a full week, and you need a break. You'd planned Saturday to be a day of rest, play, and peace. When you think of meeting these needs, a sense of lightness and relief wash over you. You realize that if you meet these needs before helping your mom, you will be able to choose from a place of generosity to help her with her project.

By not falsely placing your needs and your mom's needs in competition, you can consider her needs with care and respect. When you include the needs that are up for you as well as those up for her, you can show care and respect to both of you and to the relationship between you. Knowing that you are looking out for your own needs can create the security that allows you to attend to hers as well. If you thought that only her needs, or only your needs, could be addressed, you might feel a sense of constriction. Holding everyone's needs with care can lead to a more relaxed and generous approach.

As you feel into your needs for rest, play, and peace you get a sense of what you would like to do to nourish those needs. When you get specific with your own self-care it becomes easy to enter into negotiation with your mom. Before calling your mom you look at your calendar and choose some times in which you can easily attend to the needs for support and companionship behind your mother's request. When you get on the call you immediately start the negotiation with your specific and doable request. It might sound something like this:

"Mom, for most of the weekend I need to rest and rejuvenate from my work week. I believe I will have my energy back by late Sunday afternoon. I could come over at 3:00 and then we could have dinner together. I would want to head home by 8:00. Does that work for you?"

When you propose a plan or request that is specific and doable you naturally begin to define boundaries and invite negotiation within those boundaries. Notice how the sample proposal to mom focuses on what you are saying yes to. This moves the conversation forward into what's possible. In contrast, expressing a request in terms of what you don't want to do moves the negotiation into abstract ideas about what one should or shouldn't do, a false competition of needs, or a stalemate.

The concept of Life-Serving Boundaries is the eighth Relationship Competency in a larger framework known as Mindful Compassionate Dialogue (MCD). As with all of the 12 Relationship Competencies in MCD, Life-Serving Boundaries identifies six concrete skills for you to learn and practice. As you dive into this work with boundaries, these skills can give you a place to come back to again and again. Each time you revisit them, notice how your ability to apply them has changed and where you would like to improve.

> **WHEN YOU PROPOSE A PLAN OR REQUEST THAT IS SPECIFIC AND DOABLE, YOU BEGIN TO DEFINE BOUNDARIES**

THE SIX BASIC SKILLS OF LIFE-SERVING BOUNDARIES

1. When saying "no" to someone's request, identify the needs to which you are saying "yes"

2. Identify 3 types of useful boundaries

3. Articulate 3 non-negotiable boundaries that you hold in any relationship

4. Identify current limiting beliefs that interfere with boundary setting, and the expansive beliefs that will support boundary setting

5. Identify the signs and symptoms of behavior in yourself or others that don't support boundaries

6. Establish a boundary with body language, behavior, or words any time that you would like to change or disengage from an interaction

VISUALIZING MINDFUL COMPASSIONATE DIALOGUE

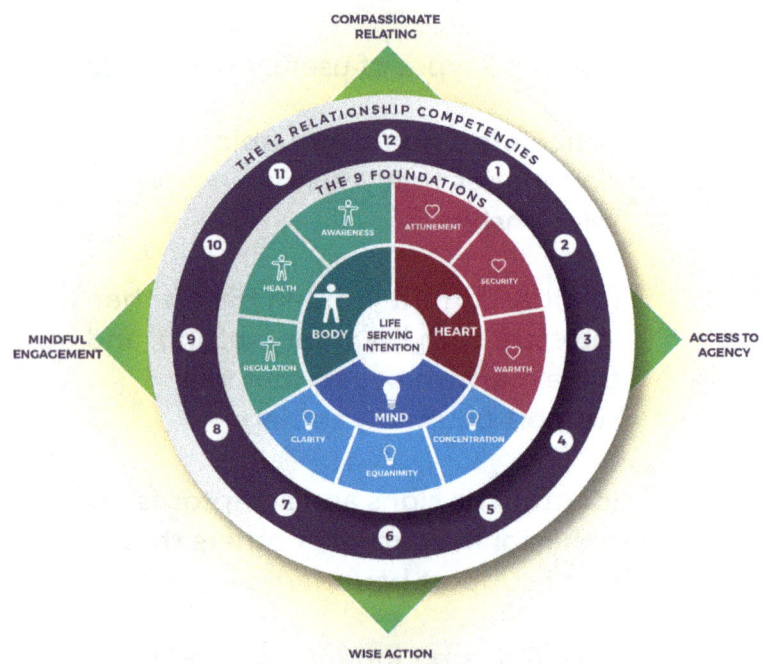

12 RELATIONSHIP COMPETENCEIS

1. Appreciation
2. Empathy
3. Honest Expression
4. Self-Empathy
5. Recognizing Reactivity
6. Managing Reactivity
7. Needs-Based Negotiation
8. Life-Serving Boundaries
9. Thriving & Resilience
10. Relationship Repair
11. Emotional Security
12. Healthy Differentiation

OVERVIEW OF
MINDFUL COMPASSIONATE DIALOGUE

Mindful Compassionate Dialogue is a system of transformation that helps people to create the relationships they want. To do that, it relies on the intention to connect and attend to present moment experience, 9 Foundations, and 12 Relationship Competencies.

The intention to connect and focus on present moment experience is key because this is where a powerful paradigm shift occurs. This shift is learning to trust that when we attain a particular quality of connection within ourselves and with another, we naturally want to engage with generosity and creativity to equally identify with care all needs present in a given situation.

The 9 Foundations are the key to working with obstacles to learning and transformation. Working with the 9 Foundations allows you to access skills when you need them most and even count on them as your natural response. These 9 Foundations are parts of yourself that you want to examine, cultivate, and strengthen. They are the foundation of your well-being—core parts of every person's emotional, psychological, and physical experience. When cultivated and strengthened, the 9 Foundations allow you to move forward and master the Relationship Competencies.

As we learn new skills, we may eventually hit a plateau where we haven't mastered the skill but can't seem to move forward. When this happens, we can examine each of the 9 Foundations for areas to strengthen or cultivate. The 9 Foundations are there because they can support us in learning and integrating the Competencies (skills) of MCD.

You could say that the 9 Foundations are places that any therapist, spiritual director, or naturopath would look to help you heal, transform, and grow.

The 9 Foundations are divided into three categories: body, heart, and mind. In the category of body I have included awareness, health, and regulation. In the category of heart—attunement, warmth, and security. In the category of mind are the elements of equanimity, clarity, and concentration.

Now let's take a look at the 12 Relationship Competencies of Mindful Compassionate Dialogue.

The 12 Relationship Competencies are a subtle and comprehensive guide for creating thriving relationships. Each Relationship Competency identifies six key skills along with specific practices for learning each skill. That's 72 skills and more than 72 specific and doable practices for learning those skills! The Relationship Competencies naturally support emotional security, while also promoting healthy differentiation. You learn to:

- Express appreciation
- Listen with empathy
- Make requests
- Access self-empathy
- Stay grounded through reactivity
- Negotiate
- Set clear boundaries
- Cultivate thriving and resilience
- Repair disconnect

Pursuing mastery of Mindful Compassionate Dialogue will increase your ability to relate to yourself and others with mindfulness, agency, wisdom, and compassion.

The framework of MCD was developed from a deep grounding in mindfulness, mindfulness-based and body-centered therapeutic modalities, and Compassionate Communication (also known as Nonviolent Communication or NVC). Let's look at each of these in turn.

NONVIOLENT COMMUNICATION (NVC)

The purpose of NVC is to create a quality of connection that inspires a natural giving from the heart. The premise of this work is that our natural state is one of compassion and connection, even though our experience of life isn't always compassionate or connected. Your experience of life may or may not match this premise, but that's okay, you can still engage with the skills.

At the center of NVC is the concept of universal needs. This is the proposal that all human beings have the same needs that they are working to nourish and be in integrity with as they go through life. Needs are "universal" because they are universally valued by people across different cultures and places. All humans, across different cultures and historical times, have the same underlying needs. Different individuals, families, and cultures may have very different ways of meeting or relating to those needs. We want to have a deep respect for this diversity of strategies, while also recognizing the universality of the values or longings that underpin them. MCD relies heavily on this concept.

Nonviolent Communication (NVC) was founded by Marshall Rosenberg in the 1960s. For more history and resources on NVC see the Center for Nonviolent Communication.

When you hear the word "need" you might associate it with an idea of lack, weakness, or neediness. On the contrary, in MCD, relating to needs is about a deep sense of self-responsibility and contributing to thriving for yourself and other living beings. Universal needs are like a guidebook for your life. Here's a very simple example. When you're thirsty, you connect with the need for water and get yourself a drink. Listening to your need and taking action from it, you contribute to your own well-being, which in turn makes you more available to contribute to others.

You can think of needs as a guiding force that lets you know where to direct your attention. Let's look at a more complex example regarding the need to be heard. Imagine you tell your partner or friend about a big success you had at work and they respond with a distracted "oh, that's nice." You feel your heart sink and a feeling of disappointment arises, alerting you that a need has not been met. Body sensations and emotions are signals that a particular need is wanting your attention.

You take a moment and ask yourself what need you were hoping to have met when you shared your news. When you name the need to be heard, you have a sense of how to get back in connection with your partner or friend. You might say something like, "I am wondering if you are available to hear this? It's big for me and I am excited to share it."

Becoming conscious of needs as they arise in the present moment is different from what I call trial and error living, in which you take action from a guess about what might work, what you have seen others do, or what someone advised you to do. Knowing exactly what needs are alive in a given situation, it is much easier to choose effective action. Sometimes connecting with a need is the effective action itself. Just experiencing the energy of a need can be nourishing and reconnect you to aliveness and alignment.

PERHAPS THE MOST REVOLUTIONARY PART OF BECOMING CONSCIOUS OF UNIVERSAL NEEDS IS

knowing that everything everyone does is an attempt to meet or align with a life-giving universal need. The more you are able to recognize this in yourself and others, the more compassion arises naturally. You find freedom from the habit of judging others and putting them in a box (e.g., nice, helpful, obnoxious, criminal, fanatic, etc.). Your ability to relate to others in a fluid and authentic way increases.

A big part of having a sense of freedom and power in your life is knowing the difference between a universal need and the strategies that meet a need. Identifying a need gives you a sense of limitless options. When you confuse a strategy for a need, or imagine there is just one strategy (or person) that can meet your need, you often feel stuck and hopeless about getting your needs met. It is also incredibly empowering to realize that needs are never in conflict. It is only an insistence that they are met in a certain way, at a certain time, or by a certain person, that creates conflict. As you cultivate creativity and flexibility about how to meet your needs, you may find that there is much less conflict in your life.

Lastly, becoming conscious of needs enables you to be deeply self-responsible. The fact is, you are already relying on others to meet your needs everyday. You are completely interdependent. To the extent that this interdependence is unconscious, you might attempt to protect or meet your needs using ineffective and harmful strategies such as withdrawing, people-pleasing, controlling, acting tough, over-working, etc.

> YOU CAN THINK OF NEEDS AS GUIDING ENERGIES

HAKOMI

Hakomi Therapy is a system of body-centered psychotherapy which is based on the principles of mindfulness, nonviolence, and the unity of mind and body. It was developed by Ron Kurtz and others at the Hakomi Institute in Boulder, Colorado.

Hakomi asks you to become ever more subtly aware of your experience and turn toward your experience with compassion and acceptance. It offers insight into universal patterns of reactivity and healing.

From the framework of Hakomi, you will recognize a set of core experiences or so-called "core material" that may exert unconscious influence on your perceptions, thoughts, beliefs, feelings, and decisions.

Core material is composed of conditioned relationships between various aspects of experience such as memories, posture, images, beliefs, neural patterns, thoughts, impulses, needs, feelings, etc. Some core material supports you in responding to life in a satisfying way, while some of it, learned in response to acute and/or chronic stress, continues to limit you (e.g., reactivity).

Hakomi offers very specific ways to use mindfulness to access core material.

As core material unfolds into conscious awareness it is met with empathy and specific healing responses, and transforms in the direction of integration and wholeness. This then changes the way you respond to life or, in other words, changes your habits, behaviors, perceptions, beliefs, and attitudes.

MINDFULNESS

Mindfulness is a quality of consciousness and kind attention. With mindfulness you are able to become aware of what goes on in you from the moment you perceive something to the moment you respond. In a single moment, you cycle through a river of thoughts, impulses, images, feelings, and needs. Shedding light on this river of experience helps you to connect to your heart and respond with wisdom and compassion.

Mindfulness is thought to have been first described and taught in ancient India before the time of the Buddha. Mindfulness is characterized by a state of mind free from greed, hate, and delusion. It is a kind and compassionate attention gently directed toward experience in the moment. It is characterized by non-forgetfulness and the absence of confusion. It arises from clear perception. In sum, it is an enhanced presence of mind, a heightened non-wavering attentiveness, and a special quality of attention.

Relative to Hakomi, mindfulness of present experience—especially experiences of the body—is the primary doorway to bring unconscious core material into consciousness so that healing can happen. It frees you from the trap of making decisions based on habits, assumptions, and limited or confused perspectives.

Mindfulness allows you to notice when you are connected or disconnected, and to direct attention toward what truly serves life.

The tables on the next two pages may be helpful for seeing where Life-Serving Boundaries fits into the framework of Mindful Compassionate Dialogue (MCD).

MCD OFFERS PRACTICAL SKILLS FOR PERSONAL TRANSFORMATION AND THRIVING RELATIONSHIPS

In this work, the quality of connection with yourself and others is the primary focus. Through cultivating the quality of connection needed in a given situation, true collaboration becomes possible.

MCD TERMS

Feelings refers to body sensations, physiological processes, and emotions that arise based on the perception (whether conscious or unconscious) of **met or unmet needs**.

Needs are universal; all human beings have the same needs. The universality of needs is a simple pathway of connection to others, providing access to shared humanity, empathy, and compassion. Integrating the vocabulary of universal needs is essential for every aspect of MCD.

Empathy is a willingness to offer curiosity and compassionate presence for another person's experience. It is distinguished by a lack of judgement or agenda for the other person.

Honest expression contains the intention to connect through shared vulnerability and self-responsibility. It often includes an observation, thought, feeling, need, and request.

Tragic strategies are behaviors that attempt to meet needs (like all behaviors), but result in more unmet needs than met needs. Our goal is to find strategies to meet needs in harmony with others.

Self-responsibility involves distinguishing universal needs from the strategies to meet them. Knowing how you meet your needs and having multiple trusted strategies to meet a single need supports emotional security, flexibility, creative collaboration, and the ability to meet your needs in harmony with others.

Reactivity is defined as the misperception of threat to one or more needs. The most obvious symptom of reactivity is contraction.

The expansive perspective refers to a state of consciousness or location within yourself in which you have access to mindfulness, skills, wisdom, an ability to consider diverse views, and a sense of connection.

MCD expresses from the consciousness of a life-serving intention. It describes 9 supportive Foundations for an integrated sense of self and 12 Relationship Competencies. Both the Foundations and the Competencies describe relational concepts and list specific and doable practices and skills. MCD manifests through compassionate relating, access to agency, wise action and mindful engagement.

THE 12 RELATIONSHIP COMPETENCIES	THE 9 FOUNDATIONS
1. Appreciation	HEART
2. Empathy	Attunement
3. Honest Expression	Warmth
4. Self-Empathy	Security
5. Recognizing Reactivity	BODY
6. Managing Reactivity	Awareness
7. Needs-Based Negotiation	Health
8. Life-Serving Boundaries	Regulation
9. Thriving and Resilience	MIND
10. Relationship Repair	Equanimity
11. Emotional Security	Clarity
12. Healthy Differentiation	Concentration

LIFE-SERVING BOUNDARIES
SKILL 1:

WHEN SAYING "NO" TO SOMEONE'S REQUEST, IDENTIFY THE NEEDS TO WHICH YOU ARE SAYING "YES"

For this skill you are being asked to move beyond knowing what you don't want and to become aware of what you do want at any given moment. You already do this when you are identifying priorities in life. Each time you identify a priority you are naturally saying no to everything that is not that. For example, when you prioritize going to the gym every Wednesday evening, you are saying no to getting together with friends, watching a movie, or doing yard work on Wednesday evening.

When you are clear about a priority in life, you likely notice a sense of solidness in yourself along with inspiration and commitment. You have a much greater sense of personal power and motivation when you are moving towards something you care about rather than away from something you don't like or want. If you enjoy going to the gym and are connected to positive feelings of health and well-being when you go regularly, it's easy for you to keep your commitment and say no to other things that come up on Wednesday evening. In this way, identifying the needs you're saying yes to when you say no to any given situation or request empowers you and helps you stand your ground. When you can easily connect to your needs in the moment, you will find that you are able to say no with a sense of security and confidence.

Keep in mind that at any given moment throughout the day you are prioritizing or saying yes to particular needs of yours, even if you are not conscious of it. This includes the need to contribute to the needs of others. For example, If you are taking care of your children, you might be saying yes to contribution and love. If you are at work, you might be saying yes to focus and efficiency, which also contributes to the needs of others.

To the extent that you are conscious of what needs you are saying yes to for any given activity, you will have a greater sense of choice and agency in your life. Needs awareness interrupts unhelpful habits of mind in which you frame your activity as something you "should" do or are obligated to do. This kind of reactive thinking blocks the opportunity to connect with true motivation. Needs awareness helps you set Life-Serving Boundaries and stay connected to yourself and others.

THRIVING

But, identifying your needs can be a little more difficult than you might expect. The concept of universal needs is not widely understood or even referred to outside of the frameworks of MCD and NVC. For the most part, people confuse preferences with needs or think about needs relative to a very short list that has been articulated by biologists and psychologists over the years. These short lists include just what you would expect: food, water, shelter, and nurturing.

When we talk about universal needs in the MCD framework, it's not just about what helps you survive but what helps you thrive. When you are only considering needs relative to survival, you are more likely to be caught in reactivity, boundary crossing, and conflict. It's difficult to know why or how to set boundaries when you are not sure what you want to protect or care for.

For example, imagine a friend is asking you for more listening than you want to give about their divorce. You know you are tired of listening, but you have difficulty setting a boundary because you are stuck in the idea that only survival needs matter. You are still able to hold a job and pay for shelter and food as you take time to listen to your friend, so why would you say no to them? This sounds a bit funny when we bring it up directly, but it is difficult to notice at the moment.

If, on the other hand, you are attuned to your needs for play, rest, support, and inspiration, you will carve out time to meet these needs. Naturally, as you attend to your needs you will not spend hours listening to your friend. When you do choose to listen, your friend will enjoy the benefit of your freely-given focused attention. When you are not as available, your friend might seek other forms of support that actually serve their needs better. They might also take a downward spiral in which they realize that they want to make major changes in their life. Ultimately though, it is important to remember that you are not responsible for your friend's decision to seek out more emotional support or to allow themselves to spiral downward. They are on their own journey, choosing their own challenges.

Thriving means that, in addition to physical needs, you attune to and care for emotional, social, and spiritual needs. It means that, in general, you function more from your brain's prefrontal cortex, allowing for rational thinking and the development of mindfulness. With this type of consistent focus you will find that you enjoy your life more and can more effectively contribute to our larger community.

ATTUNING TO UNIVERSAL NEEDS

Being able to attune to universal needs requires specific vocabulary, subtle self-awareness, and a clear understanding of the difference between universal needs, preferences, and the strategies to meet them. The easiest way to begin is to incorporate the list of universal needs into your daily vernacular.

Take a look at the following 10 specific and doable practices on the next page to help you do this. For all of these, use the list of needs provided below.

NEEDS LIST

Empathy
Intimacy
Connection
Affection
Warmth
Love
Understanding
Acceptance
Caring
Bonding
Compassion
Communion
Spirituality
Sexuality
Kindness
Gentleness

Autonomy
Agency
Choice
Freedom
Spontaneity
Independence
Respect
Honor

Security
Predictability
Consistency
Stability
Trust
Reassurance
Reliability

Partnership
Family
Presence
Mutuality
Friendship
Companionship
Support
Collaboration
Consideration
Seen/Heard
Acknowledgment
Belonging
Community
Inclusion
Participation

Purpose
Meaning
Competence
Contribution
Efficiency
Growth
Learning
Challenge
Discovery
Inspiration

Order
Structure
Clarity
Focus
Information

Appreciation
Celebration
Mourning
Aliveness
Humor
Beauty
Play
Joy

Honesty
Integrity
Authenticity
Wholeness
Fairness/Equity
Expression
Creativity

Peace
Groundedness
Hope
Healing
Harmony
Ease/Comfort
Completion

Nurturing
Food/Water
Rest/Sleep
Safety
Health
Shelter
Movement
Touch

10 SPECIFIC AND DOABLE PRACTICES

1. Buy or make a deck of needs cards. Shuffle through these cards each time you are making a difficult decision, feeling gratitude, celebrating something, reflecting on a difficult interaction, or engaging in a focused dialogue. Notice which needs resonate.

2. Memorize a list of universal needs. Without a clear vocabulary of needs, you will likely mix up needs with the strategies to meet them at the very times when it would be most useful to recognize them as separate.

3. Work backward from your strategy. That is, identify your request or the way you want something to go and ask yourself the question, "What needs will be met for me and the other person if it happens that way?"

4. Imagine the ideal scenario. See yourself in the ideal scenario or outcome of your current difficulty, and then ask what makes it ideal. What are the qualities, attitudes, and feelings present? What needs are being met?

5. Reflect on your experiences. Commit to a month of daily reflection practice. Each day, review one positive experience and one challenging experience. Use the needs list to identify what needs were up for you in each experience. If you like to write, keep a journal of your practice. Begin each daily reflection with a period of mindfulness meditation.

6. Ask for empathy. Ask someone close to you to listen to you talk about something you are struggling with for two minutes (and use a timer to stick to this limit). Then, hand them the list of feelings and universal needs and ask if they would be willing to guess what feelings and needs might be present for you regarding the situation you talked about.

10 SPECIFIC AND DOABLE PRACTICES

7 **Offer empathy.** Choose a particular relationship in which you would like to practice consistently offering empathy as your first response to the other person whenever you are together. Before you get together with them, reflect on what challenges you know this person is facing and what is most important to them. Identify the universal needs you guess are present for them in various aspects of their life.

8 **Get an empathy buddy.** Find someone who would like to practice offering and receiving empathy. Set up a regular empathy date. Use a timer for sharing and for empathy guesses. Stick to the traditional empathy guessing phrase: "Do you feel _____ because you need _____?" Use the feelings and needs list (included in the appendix) for all of your guesses.

9 **Review past relationships.** Choose a significant relationship from your past. Using the list of universal needs, make guesses about the needs you think were alive for the other person relative to the events or interactions you remember most clearly. Identify the needs that were alive for you in those moments.

10 **Use synonyms for the word "need."** Sometimes, more familiar language will give more access to identifying needs. Instead of asking "what do I need?" try asking yourself:
- "What's most important to me about this?"
- "What do I really care about here?"
- "What matters most to me about this?"
- "What do I value most?"
- "What am I committed to right now?"

EQUANIMITY WITH NEEDS

In learning to name your needs clearly and directly, you also have the opportunity to form a conscious and intentional relationship with them—ideally a relationship of equanimity. Most reactivity and decisions that lead to poor boundaries come from an unclear or insecure relationship to particular needs. (We will talk more about this with regard to Skill 4 when we address limiting beliefs.) Unfortunately, most of us have been taught to believe that some experiences are valid and others are invalid—or, in other words, some needs are okay and some are not. Beliefs like these interfere with identifying needs and knowing what's true for you.

As you read through the list of universal needs, notice any bias that comes up. You might notice an easy acceptance of certain needs, aversion to others, and complete denial of others. For example, if your family emphasized and rewarded high achievement, and you went along with this, you might easily affirm needs for efficiency, order, and competence. But you might struggle to find needs for play, community, or spirituality as equally valid. This kind of bias for competence and other achievement-related needs could translate into setting poor boundaries at work. You might find that you have set up your life in a way that leaves you chronically depleted from overworking.

Ideally, you can relate to universal needs with equanimity. You see them all as equally valid. If bias or reactivity around a particular need comes up, you can notice it and offer yourself compassion for these uncomfortable habits of heart, body, and mind. Without awareness of reactivity and bias, these habits can shape your behavior in ways that inhibit your ability to maintain Life-Serving Boundaries.

Cultivating a relationship of equanimity to your needs (or any part of your experience) is a lifelong endeavor. However, we can name three simple actions that help you cultivate equanimity:

THREE ACTIONS THAT CULTIVATE EQUANIMITY

1. Memorize the needs list so you can consistently and more accurately sort out what's happening inside. You might start by memorizing ten needs a week.

2. Cultivate mindfulness and a meditation practice so that you can more skillfully and consistently direct your attention in a life-serving way.

3. Pursue healing work to help you resolve reactivity around particular needs.

STEWARDSHIP OF NEEDS

Just as we are stewards of this earth, meant to care for its well-being, you are a steward of your own needs. Relating to your needs from the perspective of stewardship helps instill a sense of honor and respect for your own life. It interrupts common negative messages like:

- "If you make a clear request around your needs, you are being needy."
- "Good people sacrifice themselves for others."
- "You should be tough and not have any needs."
- "Don't depend on others to meet your needs. Be independent."

Messages like these are the result of confused and reactive thinking. The truth is:

- We are utterly dependent on each other.
- People who sacrifice themselves typically face chronic health problems and are often behaving from reactivity.
- As a human being you have needs and there is no way not to have them.
- When someone wants you to be "independent," they may be wanting predictability, trust, and mutuality. When you are willing to acknowledge that you depend on others to meet your needs, you can be responsible and wise about how you do that and how you contribute to the needs of others.

In addition, thinking about having stewardship of your needs reminds you that this is a communal responsibility. As you steward your needs you become a valuable member of our larger community.

> HAVING STEWARDSHIP OF YOUR NEEDS IS A COMMUNAL RESPONSIBILITY

Stewardship of needs has at least three key elements. First, it means you recognize and accept that having needs is a part of every living being's experience. Just as you wouldn't expect to drive your car without putting gas in it, you wouldn't expect to live and not attend to needs. Of course, you are always attending to your needs, it's just a matter of how conscious and effective you are about it.

Second, as a steward of your needs you understand that they are life energies that arise or come into awareness in a given context. Marshall Rosenberg, the founder of NVC, ingeniously defined the context in simple terms: Any need lives between the thing that's happening in a given moment (observation) which brings it up or makes it relevant, and the action you take to be in harmony with, attend to, or meet that need. You can choose to move in sync with this principle, grasp at it, or try to deny it. Moving in sync with it allows you to live with greater equanimity.

Third, mindful stewardship of needs gives you an opportunity to negotiate with others in a way that really works. When your relationship to universal needs isn't fraught with bias and reactivity, you can admit your utter interdependence with others and approach this with flexibility, resilience, and creativity.

PRACTICE

1. Look at your calendar for the coming week.

2. In the empty spaces on your calendar, write down the needs you anticipate that you would like to meet at those times. When you receive a request from someone or pressure yourself to do something in those spaces, check in with the needs you wrote down to see if they match the proposed request or action.

LIFE-SERVING BOUNDARIES
SKILL 2:

IDENTIFY THREE TYPES OF USEFUL BOUNDARIES

If you struggle with boundaries, making decisions about how to manage a relationship can seem like a mass of tangled thread. Sorting relationship decisions can become a disorienting process that sometimes works out and sometimes leads to another knot. You may be wanting a system for making decisions that will be simple, authentic, and alive. You want to be able to consciously choose the Life-Serving Boundary that best fits for any given moment and for any given relationship.

One approach involves getting clear about the level of contact and connection you want with the people you interact with everyday. This means knowing what you want to share, what you don't want to share, the kinds of activities you do together, and what you don't do together, etc. Deciding what level of connection you want with someone will help you set Life-Serving Boundaries to attend to other needs. For example, if you've decided to maintain less connection with a co-worker or, in other words, a distant boundary, and that co-worker asks you to come over to their house to work on a project, it would be easy to decide not to come to their house and choose a neutral location to meet instead.

When working with boundaries, you need a way to sort your experience of them. This helps you study your experience and make decisions. Sorting your decisions about boundaries into boundary types is one effective way to do this.

WE CAN DIVIDE BOUNDARIES REGARDING CONNECTION INTO THREE MAIN TYPES

1. **Distant:** in which you maintain less connection or just enough connection to complete the task at hand.

2. **Flexible:** in which you negotiate the level of connection according to what meets needs in any given context.

3. **Close:** in which you offer and invite intimate connection on a consistent basis.

SETTING A DISTANT BOUNDARY

If you hold a distant boundary in a given relationship, you share a very narrow slice of life with that person. This is common at the workplace, where sharing is limited to the work task itself. You make most relationship decisions ahead of time by deciding what to share or not share in that particular relationship or situation. A distant boundary is also sometimes necessary in family relationships. Your heart longs for family relationships that are close and supportive. When this isn't possible, you might still want to maintain some sense of connection. For example, if you experienced abuse in the relationship with your father growing up, you might choose to maintain a distant boundary. Despite the repair you have done with your father and the healing work you have done on your own, you find that there are very few things you can share with your father that create connection. Still, you want to maintain some connection. So you identify the safe topics and activities and maintain a limited relationship. Choosing in this clear way contributes to an ability to grieve the needs that won't be met with your father and find a sense of peace and acceptance about what's true in your relationship.

DISTANT: MAINTAIN LESS CONNECTION

EXAMPLE: When your coworker brings up a personal issue, you ask to return to the work task at hand.

VERBAL BOUNDARY SETTING

"I am hearing you're feeling upset about your argument with your girlfriend. So it makes sense that you want to talk about it. At the same time, I am anxious to complete this project. Are you able to focus on this right now?"

NONVERBAL BOUNDARY SETTING

Shift your body away or walk away from the other person and return to your own task.

GENERAL STRATEGIES FOR SETTING A DISTANT BOUNDARY

1. Infrequent eye contact
2. More physical space during a conversation
3. Task specific conversations only
4. Neutral facial expression
5. Limit time together
6. Contact only occurs in group settings

SETTING A FLEXIBLE BOUNDARY

In other relationships you maintain a flexible boundary. In these relationships, it's okay if sometimes there's distance and sometimes there's intimacy. You trust yourself and the other person to negotiate boundaries according to the context and needs present in the moment. You've decided that you will take the time to check in and negotiate around what is shared in any particular conversation or context. For example, you and a coworker are good friends. When you are at work you have both decided to limit your conversations to work related topics. When you meet outside of work you share freely with each other about personal topics. You shift the level of connection between you according to what the context supports.

FLEXIBLE: NEGOTIATE CONNECTION

EXAMPLE: Your sister asks you if you would be willing to take on more responsibilities in caring for your elderly mother.

VERBAL BOUNDARY SETTING

"Hmm, I am not sure if that will work. I am wanting to be effective and responsible regarding the responsibilities I already have. Would you like to talk more about it (invitation for more connection) or decide right now (invitation for action)?"

NONVERBAL BOUNDARY SETTING

An open body posture and eye contact, while standing slightly turned away, invites more connection while showing a willingness to end the interaction.

GENERAL STRATEGIES FOR SETTING A FLEXIBLE BOUNDARY

1. Check in with your own intentions, needs, expectations, and specific requests in a given context
2. Clarify the other's intentions, needs, expectations, and specific requests
3. Observe what kind of sharing or activity the environment supports
4. Pause frequently to check in with your body reactions, feelings, and needs
5. If you feel uncomfortable about a negotiation, ask to come back to it another time
6. If the other person requests something from you, create the habit of pausing before answering

SETTING A CLOSE BOUNDARY

In select relationships in your life, you maintain a close or intimate boundary. You share a lot with that person and you actively maintain intimacy. You reach towards connection, share vulnerability, and perhaps share a variety of activities together. This is the type of boundary you most often maintain with a romantic partner, close friend, or trusted family member. In a healthy relationship that maintains an intimate connection, trust has been earned through consistent experiences of respect, consideration, mutual support, honesty, and reliability.

CLOSE: MAINTAIN INTIMATE CONNECTION

EXAMPLE: You meet your friend once a week for a walk and you both share your inner challenges and gratitudes.

VERBAL BOUNDARY SETTING	NONVERBAL BOUNDARY SETTING
"I'd love to have some time, just you and me, to talk and connect."	Standing close and offering physical affection

GENERAL STRATEGIES

1. Create a space and structure that can hold an intimate conversation (e.g., ample time and private space with minimal interruptions)
2. Offer consistent support for the other's autonomy
3. Connect with present moment aliveness in both parties before addressing any specific agenda
4. Offer empathy and honest expression in turn with mindful listening and pausing to allow an organic unfolding and expression of each other's experience
5. Consistently identify what is yours to be responsible for and what is the other person's responsibility regarding feelings, needs, and resources
6. Make agreements about what is shared confidentially and what is okay to share with others
7. Clarify expectations/hopes about the amount of time you will spend together and when you will have time apart
8. Clarify what you are willing to offer each other relative to sharing, support, and contact

As you use this method of dividing types of connection into these three general categories, perhaps the most difficult thing you will encounter is times when your expectations don't match what's really needed. For example, you might long for a close relationship with your brother, but your brother doesn't have the capacity to truly hold intimacy with you in a way that meets your needs for respect and caring. If you are attached to your dream of having a close connection with your brother, you may experience hurt again and again as you invite and offer vulnerable sharing within a relationship that doesn't have the capacity to hold that vulnerability.

When you are insisting on a relationship being a particular way, your ability to see which needs can't actually be met becomes clouded. Clouded or confused thinking about this might sound like:

- I know they can meet me, they just don't want to.
- I've seen that they have this ability to love and I know they can show up.
- I won't give up on them.
- If only I can make them see...
- If only they would get a therapist then they will be able to...

Setting a distant boundary with your brother doesn't mean you are giving up on your relationship or giving up on him. It simply means that you are willing to relate in accord with things as they actually are while remaining open to change. As you grieve the relationship you wish you had with your brother, you will slowly move into acceptance of what you do have. When you make this shift, you might find that your ability to enjoy the relationship increases. When you are not longing for or insisting on something different, joy in the present naturally arises.

Discerning which of the three primary boundaries regarding connection—distant, flexible, or close—truly meets needs for you and others is a key part of bringing ease and simplicity to setting and maintaining Life-Serving Boundaries. Simply remembering that you get to choose where you stand along the continuum between close and distant with a given person can itself be empowering and help you to remember to set Life-Serving Boundaries when you need them.

> WHEN YOU ARE NOT LONGING FOR OR INSISTING ON SOMETHING DIFFERENT, JOY IN THE PRESENT MOMENT NATURALLY ARISES

PRACTICE

Reflect on relationships that already work well for you and decide which type of connection boundary you have chosen with that person. Identify all the little choices you make to maintain that helpful boundary. Studying your choices in this way will give you a better sense of what to do in a new relationship.

DISCERNING RELATIONSHIP BOUNDARIES

The table in this section is meant to reflect experience in relationships in a way that will help you discern boundaries. The organizing idea is to sort whether a given relationship is a peer relationship or not. In the larger picture of humanity we could say we are all peers. However, boundary discernment occurs in a specific context.

For example, when you are sick and go to see your doctor, your doctor is not your peer in this context. You hope your doctor went through medical school and has knowledge and expertise that you do not. This doesn't mean they're automatically in a power over position. They have a certain earned authority in their area of expertise and this is why you seek their help. Understanding power dynamics and earned authority helps you meet needs for mutuality and respect.

For instance, you might have a friendship in which that friend comes to you and consistently asks for help and you respond by consistently offering advice, comfort, reassurance, and wisdom. Over time you stop sharing vulnerably in the friendship, and you inadvertently move yourself into the position of authority in your friendship. While this might meet your need to contribute, you lose the opportunity to receive care and support. Ideally you can make a conscious decision about having a reciprocal or non-reciprocal relationship.

> IDEALLY YOU CAN MAKE A CONSCIOUS DECISION ABOUT HAVING A RECIPROCAL OR NON-RECIPROCAL RELATIONSHIP

Use the table on the next few pages to examine a particular relationship in your life in which you feel confused about setting Life-Serving Boundaries. It might be most helpful to answer these questions over several days.

TYPE OF RELATIONSHIP	
Is this a peer relationship or not? If you answer yes to any of these questions, then this is not a peer relationship. • Does one person consistently seek or give guidance or counsel? (A one-way relationship, not mutual sharing of guidance.) • Does one of you have significantly more experience within the given context? Is this the only context in which you interact? • Does one of you carry more responsibility within the context in which you interact? Is this the only context in which you interact?	**If this is not a peer relationship, consider the following:** • If you are in a position of earned authority, identify the effects of your authority and the limits of your authority. • If you are looking up to a person in earned authority, identify what exactly you are looking for and what you are not looking for; identify the limits of what you will share and what you will receive. • Are you unconsciously creating hierarchy by not sharing of yourself and/or only offering advice or, conversely, by only asking for guidance and not inquiring about the other's needs?

SUPPORTIVE CONTEXT OR CONDITIONS

What type of boundary does the situation you are usually in together encourage or discourage?

Reflect on your relationship over a given week or month. How would you usually answer these questions?

- Are others present and can they hear you?
- Is it quiet or noisy? Are you physically comfortable?
- Could you be interrupted easily?
- Is the time limited?
- Do you include or exclude others in your interaction with this person?

- Is the interaction parallel or collaborative?
- Does the shared activity or context require physical proximity or emotional sharing?
- Is it a task-focused interaction?
- Is it a service exchange interaction (e.g., doctor, dentist, mechanic, etc.)?
- What is the frequency of contact?

NEEDS AND INTENTION/EXPECTATIONS

- What needs are you and the other attempting to meet in your relationship or the situation?
- What intentions or expectations do you have for the interaction?
- Do you have a shared reality about those needs and intentions/expectations?
- Do your needs/expectations match what is actually possible in the relationship or situation?

BODY LANGUAGE

How are you and the other person holding or moving your bodies? Is body language in alignment with the boundary you want to create? The following questions may help you discern this:

- At what angle do you stand to each other?
- Are arms folded across the chest or open?
- Is there consistent eye contact or infrequent eye contact?
- What is the level of physical proximity? Do either of you lean in or away, step closer or step away?
- Do either of you relax into physical contact or tighten against it?

SHARING

- What content do you want to share and what content is not going to be shared?
- What are you willing to hear from the other and what are you not willing to hear?
- What could be shared that could trigger reactivity for you?

LIFE-SERVING BOUNDARIES
SKILL 3:

ARTICULATE THREE NON-NEGOTIABLE BOUNDARIES THAT YOU HOLD IN ANY RELATIONSHIP

When navigating any relationship, you might find yourself asking if it is okay to have particular boundaries, to decide particular behavior is a deal-breaker, or to make certain requests. You ask, "Should I expect this need to be met?" Or, "Am I supposed to be okay with this behavior?" Unfortunately the state of mind that asks questions like these is not the state of mind that can answer them. If you look for rules about what is supposed to happen or to others for advice about what boundaries you are "allowed" to set or what requests are okay to make, you only find a mess of conflicting opinions.

The truth is that you get to decide what a non-negotiable boundary is for you in any relationship. You get to decide where you want to invest your energy and where you don't. Identifying a non-negotiable boundary is about asking questions that help you understand your experience and connect with your heart. When you are connected to your heart, you ask questions that reveal what's truly nourishing and in integrity for you. You also naturally consider the impact of your decisions on others. Being present in your heart isn't about chasing romantic fantasies or trying to make everyone happy. It's about having the courage to face each moment as it is, identifying what's really true for you, and acting on that truth. An aliveness and vibrancy in your life comes from a deep sense of self-connection and knowing what truly contributes to a happy healthy life.

Collaboration and negotiation with others is the primary way we most often meet our needs. And, it is also equally important to honor the most essential ways in which you protect and care for yourself. When you find particular strategies that deeply contribute to your thriving, it makes sense that you would want to keep engaging in those. Such strategies might be called non-negotiable boundaries.

Some obvious examples of non-negotiable boundaries include sticking to particular diet restrictions, such as avoiding peanuts if you have a peanut allergy, or taking medication for diabetes if you are diabetic. Non-negotiable boundaries like these inform daily decisions. These medical non-negotiable boundaries are often easily understood and respected by others.

Non-negotiable boundaries around your emotional well-being tend to be less understood by others, primarily because they are often not communicated clearly.

HERE ARE THREE EXAMPLES OF NON-NEGOTIABLE BOUNDARIES SOMEONE MIGHT HAVE IN A CLOSE RELATIONSHIP:

1. **Consistent mutual respect:** This might mean that you refuse to maintain a relationship in which someone yells at you in anger or calls you names that you find demeaning.

2. **Willingness to repair disconnect or broken agreements:** This might mean that you won't engage in a close relationship in which the other person is unwilling to acknowledge and engage in repair when either of you behave in a way that triggers disconnect and hurt, and doesn't meet or honor needs.

3. **Support in challenging times:** One way you might define a close relationship is that the other person is willing to receive a call for help when you are in difficulty.

Let's look at an example with a student we will call Yesenia. Yesenia knows that positive judgments are a part of the general vernacular and for the most part she can hear them for what they are: people doing the best they can to say that they are enjoying her in some way. But in Yesenia's closest relationships, comments like, "You are such a sweet person," leave her bristling with reactivity. Yesenia grew up with a mom who told her who she was, what she should do, and how she should do it. This left her with a tenuous and unclear sense of self. In her closest relationships, Yesenia wants ease and care around this tender place. She wants people closest to her to take the time to find the words to express their experience in a way that doesn't include adjectives and labels of her.

If Yesenia asked other people's opinions about whether it is okay to establish a non-negotiable boundary regarding not hearing positive adjectives and labels of her, you might easily imagine the following responses from others:

- That's just the way people talk. You have to work on not taking it personally.
- You can't tell people how to talk, it's their right to say it the way they want.
- People will feel like they have to talk a certain way around you and it will inhibit their freedom.
- That's a compliment, you need to learn to take it in.
- Stop projecting your mom onto everyone.
- Other people aren't responsible for how you grew up.

Responses like these are coarse attempts to manage life with rules about what should or shouldn't happen. They effectively block a genuine response to what's true in a moment of two people interacting. Questions that direct your attention to actual experience, on the other hand, give you the information needed to discern a way forward. Here are some questions that can help you discern about whether you need to establish a non-negotiable boundary or not:

- When I am triggered, how long does it take me to manage that reactivity and come back to center?
- What kind of support would enable me to manage this trigger more effectively?
- Is there a way I can enhance the healing work I am doing regarding the needs that come up when I feel reactive?
- Am I able to learn from this reactive trigger or do I spend all my time just recovering from being emotionally flooded?
- Is the relationship nourishing enough in other ways, such that I am willing to invest energy in working with this particular trigger? Do I choose this particular challenge?
- If this person is unable to change their behavior in the way I would ask, am I willing to grieve and let go of the relationship?

When checking in with her own experience, Yesenia notices that she is not yet as effective as she would like to be at managing the reactivity that is triggered when she hears the people closest to her express a judgment of her. Thus, even when she remains silent and tries not to let it bother her, there is a significant cost. She begins to feel disconnected, distracted, and sometimes angry. Even though the other person is someone she enjoys, Yesenia feels depleted from managing reactivity rather than feeling nourished from the connection.

Yesenia realizes that she is not able to meet this challenge on her own. So, she shares her experience of the impact of hearing adjectives and positive judgments. She lets the other person know a little bit about her history and the steps she is taking to heal from that history and work with reactivity. Yesenia lets them know that while their comments are not inherently bad, the words don't work for her and asks if they have any willingness to cultivate mindfulness around not using positive judgments of her to express something they enjoy. If the other person is willing, the two of them negotiate how they could collaborate around caring for this tender place in Yesenia.

If the other person isn't willing, Yesenia may need to limit contact with this person in order to meet her own needs for peace and ease. She recognizes that becoming flooded with reactivity again and again doesn't contribute to her healing process. Yesenia finds the courage to be honest with herself about where she is in that process, what she is really able to practice and learn from, and what is too much.

This might mean letting go and grieving a relationship with someone she really enjoys; this too takes courage.

If you decide to discuss what triggers you and ask for collaboration, a certain amount of care and subtlety is needed. Several conversations may be required before the other person can connect to your tenderness rather than perceiving a threat to their needs for autonomy or acceptance. To the extent that the other person perceives a threat, doesn't have a shared experience, or is unfamiliar with the trigger, they may attempt to minimize or dismiss your concern.

You might hear them say things like:

- You're being too sensitive.
- You're making a big deal out of nothing.
- That's just me, that's how I talk. If you can't accept me...
- Just let it go and move on.
- Okay, okay, I won't say that again. Don't worry about it.
- That's not my problem.
- Those are your issues. You have to work on them.

You might feel insecure and ungrounded in the face of these kinds of responses. If so, you might back away from what you're saying, which further confuses the conversation. Learning to stay with yourself is a special kind of strength. Regardless of how the other person reacts, your experience is valid. Asking for someone to collaborate with you in taking care of your tenderness is not enmeshment or an abdication of responsibility. In fact, it is the very opposite. Direct communication and honesty about your experience, along with specific and doable requests, is self-responsibility.

When a conversation like this reaches a particular quality of connection, the other person hears your request as an invitation to contribute rather than a threat. When they hear you in this way, they can then check in with their own desire and ability to contribute in the way that you ask. Ideally, you show respect for their autonomy by releasing your request if they say no; you may then choose to end or change the relationship in a significant way.

If the other person says they are willing and able to contribute, your dialogue moves to the next stage of collaboration. For most, a simple desire to change a habitual way of behaving or speaking is not enough. Such a change requires a collaborative plan of action. This is helpful to set up before the trigger behavior occurs again. You might say something like, "This might be hard for you to remember. I'd like to find a way to remind you in a way that works for you the next time it happens. Would you be willing to brainstorm some ideas with me?"

The initial phase of learning and reminding is typically difficult. It requires graciousness on both sides; that is, a willingness to allow for a learning curve and all the little frustrations that arise when hearing something that's triggering or being asked to change a behavior. This phase depends heavily on skills in repair and requires groundedness in emotional security. This level of support and collaboration is typically reserved for close relationships in which there are many opportunities to exchange this kind of support.

In summary, relating with self-responsibility means defining non-negotiable boundaries in a specific and doable way and communicating them with the other person. When you communicate clearly, the other person can decide if it is a non-negotiable they are able and willing to respect.

When you don't communicate clearly, these boundaries are inadvertently "discovered" when they are crossed. This is a stressful way to establish non-negotiable boundaries. For example, when you happen to share some details about your partner's job with his parents, you might discover, in an unpleasant way, that your partner has a non-negotiable boundary regarding what he shares with his family of origin.

There is no such thing as an invalid or inappropriate non-negotiable boundary. You get to choose the way you would like to relate and the kind of challenges you are willing to work with in a given relationship. For example, if you have a non-negotiable boundary about only having an intimate relationship with someone who is vegan, it may limit the dating pool, but it is still your decision to make.

The key to communicating what works for you and what doesn't work for you is to make a distinction between those behaviors that are crossing non-negotiable boundaries and those that you are willing to interact and negotiate about. Of course, you might be in the process of discovering what's true for you. Sometimes this happens the hard way. For example, if you are a recovering alcoholic, you might imagine you can live with others who drink, but soon discover that you can't stay sober in that environment. No alcohol in the house then becomes a non-negotiable boundary.

Non-negotiable boundaries are set relative to what's true for you at a given time in your life. They need to be updated as you grow and change. For example, a non-negotiable boundary about alcohol in the house may shift after you have fifteen years of sobriety.

Whether you are setting life-serving non-negotiable boundaries around medical issues, emotional well-being, or physical safety, doing so depends on a foundation of secure differentiation. Let's take a look at what this means.

Complete the table on the following pages for a specific relationship or context in your life.

> **NON-NEGOTIABLE BOUNDARIES ARE SET RELATIVE TO WHAT'S TRUE FOR YOU AT A GIVEN TIME IN YOUR LIFE. THEY NEED TO BE UPDATED AS YOU GROW AND CHANGE.**

PRACTICE

Complete the following table for a specific relationship or situation in your life.

THINGS I WON'T DO OR ENGAGE WITH

THINGS I PRIORITIZE AND AM COMMITTED TO, AND WILL NOT NEGOTIATE

NEEDS I WANT TO MEET OR PROTECT IN THIS RELATIONSHIP/SITUATION

SECURE DIFFERENTIATION: STANDING IN YOUR NEEDS AND BECOMING SELF-RESPONSIBLE

Your ability to set and maintain non-negotiable boundaries will be life-giving when they arise from a secure place in yourself. I use the term "secure differentiation" here to refer to the 11th and 12th Relationship Competencies of MCD. It is a concept that describes your ability to value your own experience as valid, while respecting others' experiences as unique and valid for them. From the perspective of secure differentiation, you can hold the truth of universal needs and interconnectedness while also recognizing and embracing individual differences and unique experiences. You can deeply experience intimacy with a confidence that you won't lose yourself in another. In fact, deep intimacy isn't possible without secure differentiation.

The word "secure" in the term "secure differentiation" refers to emotional security. Emotional security is a relational confidence in which you are experiencing a felt sense of trust that you can be received and held with care by others; that all aspects of your experience are acceptable and can be met with care and comfort. With emotional security, you enjoy a predominantly confident or expansive relationship to all of your needs. You trust and know that you are innately good and worthy. You have a sense of self that is resilient and not easily threatened. This might sound idealistic and you might be wondering if anyone is emotionally secure. Rather than thinking about emotional security in binary terms (you are or you are not secure), it's more helpful to think about it in terms of a continuum. On any given day, you may be more or less grounded in emotional security.

> **EMOTIONAL SECURITY IS A RELATIONAL CONFIDENCE IN WHICH YOU EXPERIENCE A FELT SENSE OF TRUST**

The second word, "differentiation," is about celebrating and honoring differences and embracing your own uniqueness in the world. To differentiate is to decide upon the boundaries of self and create a sense of identity. Developmentally, babies are in the process of doing this when they grasp concepts like "my hand, my foot," etc. Teenagers often differentiate by distancing from their parents and trying on social identities like "the hippie," "the jock," etc. Adults often differentiate and create identity relative to a career or role in society.

At a more subtle level, from a place of healthy differentiation you can speak up even when you know others won't agree with you. You can respect another's view even when it is very different from your own. You can trust yourself to maintain a sense of self and self-care even when you relax deeply into intimacy with another. You are able to manage the reactivity or discomfort that comes from either risking greater intimacy or potential separation. This last point shows up, perhaps, most often in romantic relationships.

Differentiation could be described as being authentically who you are in the presence of who they are. If you are someone who thinks you are more connected to yourself and happier when you are not in a significant relationship, you may have developed your individuality, but likely have difficulty with differentiation. Take a look at the table below which further describes differentiation. In which of these descriptions do you see yourself? Which are things you want to explore?

CORE SKILLS & BEHAVIORS THAT SIGNIFY & SUPPORT SECURE DIFFERENTIATION

1	Groundedness and clarity about your identity, confidence in the fact of your innate goodness and lovability
2	Self-awareness, self-empathy, self-regulation/soothing
3	Self-responsibility: an ability to share unmet needs without blame, criticism, or demands
4	An ability to meet differences with respect, empathy and/or celebration
5	An ability to listen with empathy, even when the other person is upset with your behavior

6	An ability to make changes in or end unhealthy relationships
7	Consistent engagement in that which supports your thriving
8	Having multiple trusted strategies to meet any given need—that is, you don't expect to meet any need with just one person or one strategy
9	A consistent sense of meaning and purpose
10	A consistent sense of autonomy and agency
11	An ability to set life serving boundaries, and clarity about what really works for you, i.e., contributes to your thriving
12	Mindfulness practice

To understand secure differentiation more fully, it's helpful to explore examples of what it is not. Saying yes to more than you can do, staying in relationships in which someone is often unkind, or hiding away for fear of being overwhelmed by connection may all be symptoms of a lack of secure differentiation.

There are many circumstances that limit or prevent cultivation of this aspect of emotional well-being. Here are some common scenarios that don't support secure differentiation:

1. As a child, one or more of your caregivers put you in the role of being the "adult" by asking you to tend to their emotional or physical needs

2. You grew up with a sense of having to be vigilant for conflict, violence, and boundary violations

3. You were actively shamed for having feelings and needs, or your feelings and needs were ignored or dismissed

4. You were rewarded for being the "good child" and denying what was authentic for you in favor of what others wanted from you

5. You were often left alone to care for yourself; there was no one to reflect back your experience of life and offer compassion and celebration

6. You had an older sibling that you experienced as someone who attempted to establish power over you through criticism, demands, or physical intimidation/violence

If your orientation to relationships has grown out of one or more of these experiences, you likely have a sense of distrust that mutuality is even possible and doubt that your authentic experience could really be welcomed by others. These beliefs, along with needs for safety, belonging, and acceptance, drive ways of relating to yourself and others that don't support secure differentiation. Here are some examples of those unhelpful ways of relating:

1. You allow others to give you advice or information and take on the role of not knowing, when you actually do know.

2. More often than you would like, you ignore your own intuition or ideas in favor of hearing others.

3. When others have what you perceive as strong opinions or clarity about what they want, you back away from what you want.

4. You follow your attraction to others by allowing close emotional or physical contact before they have earned your trust.

5. You have some sense of giving yourself away through sex or helping others and then wonder if they have used you or will return help when you need it.

6. You assume you know what others need and offer it without checking in with them.

7. You've been told you share too much; you are not able to understand the difference between sharing authentically and adjusting your sharing to match the situation.

8. You imagine you know what others should do and give your advice without being asked.

9. You become angry and belligerent when you hear political views that don't match your own, and hear yourself frequently referring to others as idiots.

These types of habits of relating can be adaptive, growing up in a family or community that doesn't support secure differentiation. They were adaptive then, but don't meet needs for you and others now.

THREE AREAS OF REFLECTION

The healing and skills that help with secure differentiation are subtle, numerous, and varied. For our purposes, let's look at three areas for specific reflection and practice:

1. INTERRUPT "HELPING"

Notice your impulse to offer help, get involved, or give spontaneous counseling or advice. True help for others is a response to their needs and requests. In the case of a lack of secure differentiation, helping others is often a response to your own needs for connection, belonging, acceptance, and inclusion. Helping that comes from this place is often contains an unconscious "give to get" intention that is not about true mutuality.

Next time you notice the impulse to help, give advice/counsel, or get involved, pause. Take a physical step back from the other person or group. Balance your weight over your center. Follow a full breath in and out. Invite yourself to calmly observe and notice if anyone is asking for your help or involvement and, if so, what exactly are they asking for? Respond to requests for help or involvement by saying that you will get back to them later. When you are not in that situation, connect with your needs and priorities and decide what is really true for you.

2. MONITOR EYE CONTACT

You get to decide where your attention and energy flows. Love and compassion isn't about smiling at and connecting with everyone. Long uninterrupted eye contact invites intimacy before it has been earned. Take time to reflect on your choices about eye contact next time you are in a group. Ask yourself who has earned your trust through kindness and respect. Identify those you may feel a pull towards, but who have not earned such trust. Identify those who have behaved in ways that have not met your needs in the past. Make a decision, just for that event, about with whom you will allow extended, brief, or no eye contact.

3. MONITOR PHYSICAL INTERACTION

Physical interaction is much more than touch. It also includes body posture, following someone, walking with someone, proximity, hand gestures, and facial expressions. When there is touch, notice the length, the frequency, the amount of body contact, stiff or relaxed body, and if the contact moves or is stationary. The presence or lack of these things define the boundary between you and the other person.

Choose two relationships in your life. Choose one in which you have a sense of safety and predictability, but the relationship may or may not be intimate. Choose another in which you have some confusion about boundaries. You might have labeled touch in that relationship as "creepy" or you might find yourself wanting more touch while having a thought that you shouldn't want more. In each relationship, examine what supports the boundaries you want and what doesn't.

LIFE-SERVING BOUNDARIES
SKILL 4:

IDENTIFY CURRENT LIMITING BELIEFS THAT INTERFERE WITH BOUNDARY SETTING AND THE EXPANSIVE BELIEFS THAT WILL SUPPORT BOUNDARY SETTING

Before jumping into an examination of limiting and expansive beliefs, it's essential to acknowledge the influence of experiences in your family or origin.

If you have difficulty setting boundaries, there's a good chance that you grew up in a family where setting a boundary (asking for something outside the family norms, saying no, or attempting to make a decision for yourself) was punished, shamed, or simply ignored. As a kid, your first imperative is to belong to your parents and family. This is a deeply wired response that is meant to ensure your survival. In order to maintain a sense of safety and belonging, you might have walled off parts of yourself, sending particular needs into exile. As an adult, this leaves you with the mistaken impression that you don't have a right to certain needs, or that those needs are somehow "bad."

These walling-off behaviors can be very difficult to change. An attempt to change them triggers the fear experienced in the original traumatic situation. This sense of threat implores you to stop what you are doing, and to back away at any cost or to fight at any cost. Your heart starts pounding, your palms sweat, and adrenaline rushes through you. Your body tells you to flee or fight the threat and return to a calm state as soon as possible. Really though, you are lucky if your symptoms are this obvious, because it's easier to see how the reaction doesn't match the situation and to realize this when you reflect on the situation later.

What's more common is that you have adopted a set of complex decision making processes that keep you from ever facing the same threat. You learn which situations to avoid and how to navigate through potentially threatening situations in such a way that the sense of threat remains minimal.

So, in learning to set Life-Serving Boundaries you may be faced with two fundamental challenges:

TWO FUNDAMENTAL CHALLENGES

1. The ability to mindfully and compassionately meet acute, heart pounding reactivity that occurs when you move forward with setting a boundary in what you perceive as a threatening situation

2. The capacity to wake up to all the unconscious ways you sacrifice who you are in order to avoid a potential threat to one or more needs

Recognizing Reactivity and Managing Reactivity are the 5th and 6th Relationship Competencies of Mindful Compassionate Dialogue. Studying and integrating these Competencies, you can learn to mindfully and compassionately meet reactivity. Until you can do this effectively, reactivity may lead to defensiveness, blaming or judging the other person ("They're wrong!"), collapsing into self-blame ("I'm wrong!"), or disengaging through alcohol, comfort foods, or distraction. Thus, investing in learning to recognize and manage reactivity is an essential part of setting Life-Serving Boundaries.

Being able to maintain self-connection and express yourself authentically requires a subtle study of your experience, decisions, and results of those decisions. Watch for the following signs of abandoning yourself. Each one is a cue for engaging in self-empathy or asking for empathy from another.

- A sense of shrinking
- "Puffing up"—trying to be the one in charge, with a sense of self-righteousness
- Accusing others of taking advantage of you, using you, or ignoring you
- Feeling disconnected
- A sense of inauthenticity as you attempt to give empathy or achieve harmony
- Regret or pain about not getting what you really want
- Complaints about how others get what they want but you don't
- Judging someone as selfish for engaging in self-care and saying no to what they don't want or asking for what they do want
- Noticing that you have very few friendships or that friendships don't last or feel close

As you see reactivity clearly and meet it with compassion, you will become more free to make the choices that serve you and others. To begin to change your relationship to boundaries at this level, it's important not only to watch for reactivity, but to also look for opportunities to set boundaries in situations in which you feel secure.

For example, you might practice setting boundaries with a trusted friend. You may say no to his idea about where to eat; you may ask for what you want even if you feel uncomfortable doing so. As you set these little boundaries in secure relationships, mindfully take in the others' responses and notice with your whole body that you are safe and nothing bad is happening.

BOUNDARY TYPES IN FAMILY OF ORIGIN

To help you reflect on your patterns, I have identified some of the common behaviors in families according to types of boundaries that are generally healthy or life-serving, and types of boundaries that are generally not life-serving (enmeshed, disengaged, and hyperflexible—these terms are more fully described in Skill 5).

Enmeshed: In a family with no sense of boundaries/enmeshed boundaries you might find the following:

Sexual abuse, criticism, parents have agendas for their child, child runs the house, chaotic coming and going of various members, addiction, putting child in a parental role, projection of parent experience onto a child (if parent always wanted to play the violin growing up then the child must play the violin), parent needs are not distinguished from child's needs, child is left unattended (neglect), power dynamics are unpredictable

Disengaged: In a family with disengaged or rigid boundaries you might find the following:

Parent makes demands, inflexible routines, scripted beliefs and philosophies, static roles, limited access to information, communication that follows a script—some things allowed and others not, limited ability to negotiate, action comes from duty, obligation, and tradition, right/wrong thinking

Hyperflexible: In a family with hyperflexible boundaries you might find the following:

There is a sense of chaos as parents change what they are doing to please someone else; there may be a chronic problem of over-committing, resulting in a general lack of emotional resiliency, physical exhaustion, and illness; kids may rule the house with impulse and whim

Healthy: In a family with Life-Serving Boundaries you might find the following:

Roles are defined, predictable and negotiated explicitly; needs are consistently named and met, or when unmet that experience elicits compassion from other family members; agreements are transparent and explicit; rules are made for the purpose of ensuring that needs are met; parents meet their own needs with and separate from the family setting; rules and agreements match the developmental stage of the child

EXAMPLE: BOUNDARIES IN FAMILY OF ORIGIN WORKSHEET

The purpose of this exercise is to help you make the connection between your needs and how you set boundaries regarding them.

Look at the boundary types. Which of these do you see operating in your family of origin today?

BOUNDARY TYPES

Enmeshed	Hyperflexible	Disengaged
I hear my mom tell my sister that she's depressed because her kids don't live with her.	I hear my older sister say to another sister, "I will just do what everyone else wants to do."	My dad didn't tell us he had surgery.

Below are needs that someone may have been trying to meet with the strategy above.

NEEDS THAT MIGHT HAVE BEEN PRESENT

For Mom	For older sister	For Dad
connection love companionship support family	safety harmony peace acceptance	privacy security choice

In the table on the next page, identify moments when you witnessed a family member engage in enmeshed, hyperflexible, or disengaged boundaries. Write an example for each, and then guess the needs they might have been trying to meet or protect in that moment. Lastly, identify potential new strategies to meet these same needs in a way that is life-serving.

BOUNDARIES IN FAMILY ORIGIN WORKSHEET

BOUNDARY TYPES		
Enmeshed	Hyperflexible	Disengaged

NEEDS THAT MIGHT HAVE BEEN PRESENT

NEW LIFE-SERVING STRATEGIES FOR MEETING THESE NEEDS

WHAT ARE LIMITING AND EXPANSIVE BELIEFS?

Your beliefs about life, yourself, and others are an incredibly powerful part of how you make decisions and orient yourself to life. Identifying, understanding, and transforming beliefs is an essential part of the personal transformation process.

Beliefs are something that you learn little by little through various experiences. Limiting beliefs are those beliefs that were formed under painful circumstances. A limiting belief is a sort of generalization. Because you had a particular set of experiences, you tell yourself a story that all of life or some aspect of life is a certain way. Typically the most influential limiting beliefs are those that were formed in early childhood, from birth to age seven. Unless they are identified and worked with consciously, these limiting beliefs will continue to influence you even though they no longer match your life experience. It requires a consistent intention and new experiences to change them and integrate new beliefs. The first step is just to become aware of them.

The next page has a list of common limiting beliefs regarding boundaries. As you read each of the limiting beliefs listed, notice if you experience any sense of familiarity or resonance with particular ones. If one sounds familiar, use the space provided to rewrite it until it matches one of your own limiting beliefs.

LIMITING BELIEFS

Beliefs that your safety depends on either hyperflexible boundaries or rigid boundaries	Beliefs that you can't have both authenticity and belonging	Belief that to avoid being abandoned, you must create a close boundary, share early and often, and get others to do the same
"I can only be safe if I please you."	"If I am authentic, you will go away."	"I have to create closeness quickly to keep you from going away."
"I can only be safe if I keep my distance."	"If I want to be in this relationship or group, I can't be myself. I have to be a certain kind of person to belong."	"To keep from losing you, I have to constantly attend to our connection."

Once you've identified a limiting belief, the next step is to catch it in action. Where is it showing up? What are the clues that it is operating? Here are some common signs that limiting beliefs are affecting your capacity to set Life-Serving Boundaries:

- Feelings of resentment, deflation, or numbness after making a decision or agreement
- Keeping a scorecard (e.g., "I did that with you so you should do this with me.")
- A sudden feeling of dislike or hate for someone close to you
- Anger outbursts that seem to come from nowhere
- Asking for alone time more than you ask for connection time
- Feeling desperate to repair a rupture in connection or to keep someone close
- Saying "yes" to something and then blaming others for pressuring you into the decision
- Demanding that others do things for you

> **LIMITING BELIEFS HAVE LESS POWER WHEN YOU CAN SEE AND HEAR THEM MORE CLEARLY**

Once you start noticing these beliefs in action, either state them aloud or write them down. Limiting beliefs have less power when you can see and hear them more clearly. Saying them aloud in a trusted relationship is a helpful strategy. For example, imagine your partner has asked you to go to dinner with their parents on Friday. You don't really want to go but you hear yourself say yes anyway. You notice a limiting belief is triggering a sense of pressure to say yes.

To help free yourself from the grip of this belief, you might say something like: "I hear myself saying yes to your request, and I notice this old belief in the back of my mind telling me that I have to say yes to all your requests in order to be loved by you. I don't really believe that. I don't want to make decisions from that old belief. I trust that I can communicate my needs and negotiate a way for both of our needs to be met. I'm wondering if you could help me brainstorm ways I could meet my need for rest and still contribute to your need for family this week?"

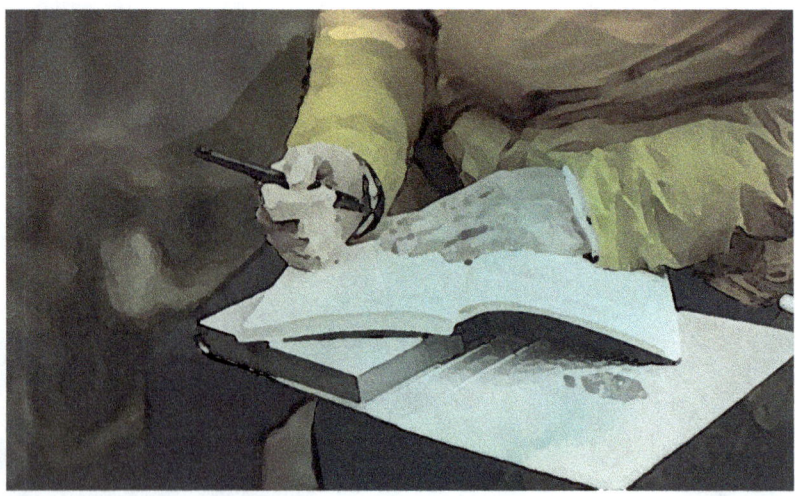

Immediately taking responsibility for your inner struggle by making a specific and doable request, ("...could you help me brainstorm..") opens the door for collaboration. Just sharing the limiting belief doesn't provide a new way forward and may lead to a conflict in which the other person perceives criticism or imagines they have to be your therapist or somehow fix the situation. True collaboration means you put your needs on the table, invite the other person to do the same, and then express and negotiate requests.

It's difficult for a limiting belief to keep its hold on you when you bring it into the light of compassionate awareness. Ideally, you are able to do this in a dialogue with another. If that approach is not available to you, then bringing it into awareness through journaling or work with a therapist is a helpful alternative.

You can work more with limiting beliefs and reactive boundaries in the table on the next page. The first row contains an example.

CONNECTING BOUNDARIES TO BELIEFS AND NEEDS

Practice with your own examples of reactive boundary setting.			
With who or in what context	Boundary type & your behavior	Limiting belief	Needs you are attempting to protect
In social settings with unfamiliar people	Hyperflexible: I sometimes say yes to requests before checking in with myself	"I can only be safe if I please you."	Safety, harmony

It's equally, if not more, important to identify expansive beliefs about boundaries. Often you can articulate these by considering the opposite of the limiting belief. You are likely operating out of an expansive belief a good portion of the time. It's just about becoming aware of that. Take a look at the list of expansive beliefs below and consider situations in which your behavior shows that you are operating from an expansive belief.

EXPANSIVE BELIEFS

1. I can express caring for your needs without having to meet them.

2. I can express the needs of mine that wouldn't be met if I said yes to your request.

3. I can support you in getting your needs met without me being the one to meet them.

4. I can ask if there are other ways I could meet your needs that would also allow me to meet my needs.

5. I am worth taking care of.

6. Taking care of my needs is a service to others.

7. Setting clear boundaries creates healthy relationships.

8. I can set boundaries and be loved.

9. I can set boundaries and be safe.

10. I can be authentic and be accepted.

UNDERSTANDING THE LIMITING BELIEFS OF ENMESHMENT

When you think about standing in your truth, your thoughts might turn to supporting particular social justice or political actions. If this is true, then you likely have worked hard to identify what you think will truly be of service to the greater community. You've developed a part of yourself that speaks out and takes action in these realms.

And yet, when it comes to a particular personal relationship, you might find that you are losing yourself. You let things slide or try to harmonize when someone is behaving in a way for which you would set boundaries in any other context. You are shocked when someone points it out because you value respect and consider yourself to be an outspoken person with good boundaries. How can this be happening? What happens in this one aspect of your life that causes you to show up differently?

The most common trigger for this anomaly is that the relationship somehow mimics a situation from your family of origin. For example, imagine that you have experienced a feuding pattern of relating in your family of origin. Often in this pattern, family members fight and argue and then don't speak to each other for years. Imagine that you moved to the other side of the country in an attempt to extricate yourself from this dynamic, but somehow you now find yourself in a very similar situation at work. It's so similar that you can name the roles each person is playing—your coworker is playing the part of your aunt who says one thing to one person and something different to another, your supervisor is playing the part of your mom who overworks and then blames others for it, etc.

> ...YOU NOW FIND YOURSELF IN A VERY SIMILAR SITUATION AT WORK... IT'S SO SIMILAR THAT YOU CAN NAME THE ROLES EACH PERSON IS PLAYING

In situations like these, it is all too easy to find yourself in your own family of origin role. The reactive dynamics of family sweep up each person into an unconscious enactment. While it seems like this is your family enactment, it's likely that it also represents someone else's family. This is what makes it incredibly difficult to use all of the skills, consciousness, and strengths that you've cultivated. Seeing the reactive pattern clearly, you have a chance to wake up from your family trance. You can locate yourself in the strengths and skills you've cultivated and bring them to this particular relationship. Let's look at a few practical steps to achieve this.

The first step, as you might have already guessed, is getting empathy for yourself from someone outside of the situation. Ideally, this person can help you see the situation more clearly by taking the following steps: reflecting back your observations, thoughts, feelings, and needs; compassionately naming the patterns they see; and affirming the validity of your needs and the truth of your skills and strengths. This affirmation helps you wake up out of the family trance.

The most common element in any family trance is enmeshment—a lack of adult differentiation. In your care and compassion for another person, you imagine, from within the family trance, that if only you did the right thing you would be able to change their perspective and behavior. You imagine that somehow you can regulate their emotions (for example, by helping them stay calm or keeping them happy) and then they will treat you in a way that you enjoy. This is an example of enmeshment.

It's essential to see all the way through this delusion and release it completely. Seeing through delusion is often a process of naming and observing all of the ways you enact it. You can make a list in your journal or talk it through with a compassionate friend. The important piece is that you have very specific behaviors and thoughts to watch for in yourself and interrupt. Each time you interrupt the pattern of enmeshment, you can use a tool you have for coming back to center and then set a boundary.

> IT'S ESSENTIAL TO SEE ALL THE WAY THROUGH THIS DELUSION AND RELEASE IT COMPLETELY

What you do inside yourself to set a boundary is the same in any situation. It's about becoming very clear about what matters most. This necessitates releasing your judgments, analysis, and "shoulds" regarding the other person. As long as your focus is on why they do what they do or how they should or shouldn't behave, you can't get clear about yourself. Whenever a student asks me for help regarding a particular relationship and they talk much more about the other person than themselves, I consider it a sign that they are likely caught in enmeshment. Focusing on the other person is not only a distraction from self-connection, it is also a sign that you are still caught up in the idea that if only you understood them enough and did the right thing, you could change them. When you completely release this idea, you naturally attend to your own needs and speak from what is important to you.

Let's look at some possible boundary setting behaviors. What a boundary looks like or sounds like depends on the context of your relationship with the other person. For the sake of these examples, let's imagine the other person is a coworker at the same level as you in the hierarchy of responsibilities at work:

SETTING A BOUNDARY TO INTERRUPT SOMEONE TRYING TO GET YOU TO TAKE SIDES

Coworker: "I can't believe John didn't follow these instructions. Now I have to go over his work! Don't you think …"

You: "Tricia, I feel very uncomfortable talking about John when he's not here. Could you speak to him directly? Do you want to talk about the project we're working on together?"

SETTING A BOUNDARY TO INTERRUPT TALKING ABOUT PEOPLE WHEN OTHERS ARE IN EARSHOT (BROADCASTING)

(Employees that you supervise are within earshot.)
Coworker: "I can't believe how many times I have to tell them. They keep..."

You: "I hear your frustration and I value respect and focus for our staff. If there is something you need to discuss, let's bring it up at the staff meeting on Friday."

SETTING A BOUNDARY TO INTERRUPT PERSONAL CRITICISM

Coworker (in a volume above average conversational volume): "You spent way too much time on this project! You can't seem to…"

You: "Hang on Alex, let's pause." (In an initial matching volume). "I don't want to talk with you at that volume. Would you be willing to lower your voice volume and tell me what your request is, rather than what you think I am doing wrong?"

SETTING A BOUNDARY TO INTERRUPT A HARSH TONE OF VOICE

Coworker: "I have to do everything around here. Nobody can get it right. If people would just listen…"

You: "Sadie, wait. I feel tense when I hear your tone of voice. I want peace in our workplace. Would you be willing to shift your tone and tell me how I can help right now?"

Notice in these examples how each response to the coworker includes either a feeling, need or implied need, and then a direct request. When you are making a request, it's important to know what you will do if the other person escalates or says no. It is in this moment of escalation that you may be tempted to revert to the old habits. Escalation by the other person is neither a "yes" nor a "no" to your request; it simply signals an inability to engage in negotiation. Of course, you are in the position of discerning what constitutes escalation.

Here are some typical signs of escalation:

- Criticism about your request: for example, "You think everyone has to do it your way."
- Name-calling: "Damn, what are you so uptight about?!"
- A "why" question such as, "Why do you think I'm upset about this?!"
- Defending their behavior: "I can talk however I want to. You don't have any idea…"
- Attacking you: "Do you think you're perfect?! You raised your voice last Friday!"
- Accusations of "power over" or arrogance: "You just think you're a perfect communicator because you've taken those classes. Well I say things honestly…"

> **IT'S IMPORTANT TO KNOW WHAT YOU WILL DO IF THE OTHER PERSON ESCALATES OR SAYS NO**

It is highly probable that the other person will escalate in response to your request or boundary. If a particular reactive dynamic is expected in which you previously tried to calm them down or harmonize, the other person will unconsciously seek to return to that dynamic. Boundary-setting can seem to make things worse at the beginning. During this phase of change, standing in your truth is essential. The list of escalating symptoms above will hopefully cue you to return to your experience, rather than being pulled into defending or engaging the content of what the other person is saying. To maintain your boundary, you can simply walk away or repeat your statement and request. When the other person sees that they cannot hook you into the old dynamic, they may make a resentful comment and walk away themselves. Of course, they may escalate further. It's important for you to walk away before your nervous system shifts you into freeze, fight, or flight mode. You want to teach yourself that you can walk away while still maintaining your boundary, rather than walking away out of fear.

As you stay self-connected in the face of a challenging relationship, you break with the legacy of your family in which feuding or stonewalling (refusing to engage) was the solution to conflict. You stand in the possibility that you can stay connected in your heart while communicating your feelings, needs, requests, and boundaries, and while knowing that even though you invite the other person into connection, you can never control how they will respond or what they will do.

PRACTICE

Take a moment right now to reflect on an example in which you stayed with your needs and requests instead of becoming hooked into a familiar reactive dynamic. What did it feel like to do that? What did you remember or believe in that moment? What forms of external support were present? How did you support yourself in doing that?

POWER DYNAMICS AND LIMITING BELIEFS

Much pain and suffering comes from confusion about the difference between authority and power over. In an ideal world, someone who is in authority has earned that authority through experience and learning. For example, your boss has a certain authority at work. She is likely able to hold a big picture of what is happening with the business and its employees and what needs to happen. She has earned this authority through work experience and education. Because of this earned authority, you and your co-workers give more weight to her ideas, decisions, and directives. You trust what she is doing most of the time in regard to work decisions.

But when you give your boss authority in areas other than the immediate work environment or when you trust her every decision without checking in with your own sense of integrity, you are moving into a "power over"/"power under" consciousness. For example, your boss doesn't get to weigh in on whether it is healthy for you to take an extra shift this week or not. Only you have authority over your own self-care.

Let's take a look at three ways to talk about power and the associated beliefs or ideas in each.

"Power with" refers to a life-serving consciousness in which the needs of all life are considered with respect and care. In a "power with" consciousness, you maintain awareness and responsibility for your needs and values while being able to consider and hear the needs of others. You have a willingness to use your internal and external resources to honor all needs present. When you receive guidance and directives from someone in authority, you are able to discern your response in integrity with your needs/values and all the details relevant to that context. If something seems off, you are able to ask questions of the person in authority. You have clarity about the boundaries of this person's authority. You remember that the needs of all are equally important regardless of roles and responsibilities.

Here are some signs that you are relating from "power with" consciousness:

11 SIGNS & SYMPTOMS OF "POWER WITH"

1. You work to stay grounded in compassion in the face of difficulty or conflict.

2. You engage openly about needs and strategies to meet needs.

3. You consistently shuttle your attention back and forth between the needs of another and your own.

4. You trust that mutual care and respect for both your own needs and the needs of others will create a quality of connection that leads to effective and creative collaboration.

5. When you follow a directive, you are clear about your own choice to say yes and what needs will be met.

6. You can offer empathy just as easily to someone above you in a hierarchy as you can to someone below you in a hierarchy.

7. When making decisions that affect others, you seek out collaboration in the decision making process.

8. You consider the needs of others equally without regard to rank, age, or other differences.

9. When you encounter a conflict, you can engage in negotiation with respect for differing perspectives. That is, you don't resort to criticism, convincing, manipulation, or just shutting down.

10. You recognize the limits of your own cultural perspective and get curious about how to include differences so that all needs can be honored.

11. You can offer empathy without taking responsibility for the other person's needs.

"Power under" in the context of MCD refers to a reactive state of consciousness fueled by limiting beliefs and tragic behaviors. In "power under" consciousness, you give away your power and hold your own needs as less important than those of people you have put in power over you. You might choose to do this to protect needs for safety, security, support, or belonging.

At the systems level, individual choices are conditioned by a matrix of interdependent relationships, and sometimes these systems have more momentum than any one individual can challenge. This is oppression rather than "power under," though both may be present for any given individual.

Our focus here is on the small scale of interpersonal relationships and the ways in which you can access your individual power/agency. Here are some signs that you are relating from "power under" consciousness:

13 SIGNS & SYMPTOMS OF "POWER UNDER"

1. You make decisions more often based on what others may approve of rather than on what feels right for you.

2. You believe your needs are not as important or you don't deserve to have them met.

3. You don't speak up when something is happening that violates your ethics.

4. You ask for or willingly receive advice from someone about areas of your life outside of the dimension in which they have authority.

5. You bend your sense of personal boundaries to accommodate another's wishes.

6. You lose access to the whole of who you are and your own sense of what is true in the presence of someone you see as having power over you, as if you were in a trance.

7. You feel smaller, speak in a smaller voice, or literally make yourself smaller through posture.

8. After talking to the person you put in "power over," you feel confused or fuzzy, or disconnected from yourself.

9. You lose your sense of humor and creativity.

10. You imagine you don't have a choice.

11. You "can't say no."

12. You see your own pain and suffering through the eyes of judgment, as things you caused or deserved, rather than through the eyes of compassion, as experiences of being human and things that indicate universal needs are wanting some attention.

13. Either implicitly or explicitly, you agree to keep secrets regarding activities that may violate moral or ethical standards.

As with "power under," **"power over"** also is a reactive state of consciousness fueled by limiting beliefs and tragic behaviors. When you come from a "power over" consciousness, you are likely confused about the boundaries of your earned authority. You may have also been seduced by opportunities for ego building, the adrenaline rush of perceived power, or pressure from others to show strength through "power over" strategies. You may be attempting to meet the same needs as the person who is coming from a "power under" consciousness: safety, security, support, or belonging. If you occupy a privileged role in the larger culture, you will have more access to resources and power, but may not be aware of power dynamics. Because of conditioning you will likely have to work hard to stay in "power with."

15 SIGNS & SYMPTOMS OF "POWER OVER"

1. You believe your needs are more important or you deserve to have them met before others.

2. You give less attention and consideration to those you perceive as lower than you in a hierarchy.

3. You unilaterally make decisions that will impact others.

4. You announce what is going to happen rather than negotiate to consider the needs of others.

5. You give unsolicited advice about things not falling in your area of authority.

6. You become angry and resentful if someone doesn't follow your advice or do things in a way you expect.

7. You view the other as incapable, pitiful, and in need of rescuing.

8. You imagine you know what is right for another without asking them.

9. You often think about what a person or group of people should and shouldn't do.

10. You blame, shame, praise, and criticize.

11. You ask someone that you perceive to be lower in the hierarchy to do personal favors for you outside of their role or job description.

12. You are willing to have your needs met at the cost of someone else's needs.

13. You regard someone's pain and suffering as something they cause or deserve, or as a lesson for them to learn, rather than relating with compassion and empathy.

14. You punish others.

15. You ask someone, implicitly or explicitly, to keep secrets that might harm others.

HOW TO SHIFT FROM DEMANDS TO REQUESTS

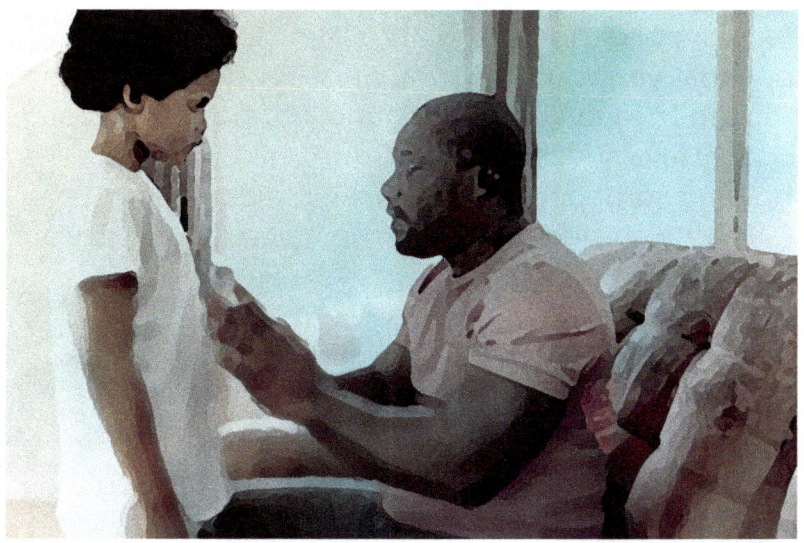

You might start to panic when, even after you have worked so hard to be clear and conscientious in your communication, your partner still doesn't offer what you are longing for. You have been diligent about sharing your needs and making clear requests, and you don't know what else to do. In this situation, panic and desperation can turn into making demands.

A demand is defined by an attempt to meet your needs at the expense of someone else's needs. It may take the form of direct verbal communication. This is the most common understanding of demand. I want to expand the definition of demand to include manipulation which is another form of attempting to meet your needs without consideration of the other person's needs.

Demands are characterized by thoughts like, "They should do this!" Or, "This has to happen!" There is a closing off of creativity and openness to other strategies. You may try to stimulate guilt, shame, fear, or obligation in the other person to get them to do what you want, and you are not open to hearing "no." In the worst-case scenario, physical use of force occurs like: shoving, hitting, slamming doors, holding someone down, blocking a doorway, following someone around the house when they are trying to leave, etc.

In everyday life, demands take the form of subtle manipulation that don't always get identified as such. For example, possibly the most pernicious form of manipulation is an attempt to get someone to do something under the pretense of helping. Often this includes an analysis of what's wrong with the other person. You may have had this experience. Your partner begins pointing out, in a subtle way with sophisticated vocabulary and jargon, how you are failing, what's wrong with you, or why your own experience isn't valid. Typically this is hard to catch as some bits of truth are often present such as specific observations. You likely walk away from such an interaction feeling depleted and disoriented with thoughts of self-doubt.

A more common form of demand is an attempt to convince someone of another point of view without asking if they are open to change. Underlying this is the idea that you are right and they are wrong and if only they could see it your way, then your needs would be met. Convincing can take many forms: yelling, logical arguments, criticism, gathering evidence for your case, etc.

Any form of demand prevents you from being present with the truth that something is fundamentally not working for you about your relationship. Sadly, as you avoid this truth, the likelihood that you can work through it lessens.

True requests involve these elements: (1) a willingness to hear "no," and (2) maintaining connection to the needs of both people, including the need for autonomy in the person receiving the request. Such honesty with yourself and the other person bring both people closer, as there is an increased sense of vulnerability, choice, and respect, held within an awareness of interdependence. In addition, true requests are about a specific doable behavior at a specific time to nourish a particular need.

The best way to prevent making demands is to find a willingness to grieve that you have not yet found a way to meet your needs. In the instant before a demand arises, there is grief and a longing for something different.

As you allow grief, the energy of life can move and flow. Grief has its own life. Your responsibility is to create space for it to unfold. When grief flows purely there are no words or stories, just a wave of sadness. Allow the waves of grief; when it comes, it comes; when it arises, it arises; and when it dissolves, it dissolves.

We can call grief and mourning the process of consciously connecting with the pain of loss. There are many forms of loss. Here are a few:

- The loss of a loved one or material thing
- Not having the connection you want with the other person
- Not being able to meet specific needs with a particular person
- Not fulfilling a particular dream
- Key moments in life when you wished a certain person was with you in a specific way
- A type of relationship you wished you had with a particular person

The mourning you do not allow can keep you stuck in anger or bitterness and repetitive conflicts.

Suffering arises from resistance to what is. This usually includes thoughts about what should or should not be. Allowing grief and mourning helps you accept what is and connect with the beauty of your needs—what is important to you in a particular situation. From there, you may discover some new strategies for meeting those needs. In doing so, you liberate yourself from the limitations of being attached to only one strategy for meeting your needs.

You can gain confidence with grief by looking for small moments of disappointment in your day. For example, maybe you are hoping for an email response from someone and when you open your inbox, it isn't there. You can pause for one full breath and say to yourself, "Oh, I feel sad about not seeing the email." Then put your attention on the feelings of sadness, no matter how small. You might be surprised how quickly they dissolve with your mindful attention. Without the proliferation of associated thoughts, grief has its own natural life, arising and falling away. Rather than demanding that life or another person shape itself according to your wishes, grief teaches you to trust in the natural flow of change and opens the door to wisdom.

PRACTICE

This week, set your intention to pause when you notice moments of disappointment or sadness. When you do, say to yourself, "It's okay to feel this sadness." Pause for three breaths and give your full attention to grief, no matter how small. Look for the sensations of grief in your body and focus on them without any accompanying thoughts. Just let your bare attention rest on grief and notice how it moves.

LIFE-SERVING BOUNDARIES
SKILL 5:

IDENTIFY THE SIGNS AND SYMPTOMS OF BEHAVIOR IN YOURSELF OR OTHERS THAT DON'T SUPPORT BOUNDARIES

Part of cultivating the skill of Life-Serving Boundaries means setting yourself up for success. This means engaging in environments and relationships that offer support and respect for your boundaries and leaving or changing the ones that don't. To do this you want to be able to recognize a boundary crossing when it happens. This includes recognizing relevant body sensations, thoughts, impulses, energy, and feelings that tell you a boundary is being crossed.

In this section, you will learn about the core concepts of enmeshment and disengagement. You will also learn to identify key differences between:

- Accommodating others from your heart versus abandoning your needs
- Entering into negotiation versus convincing or submitting to pressure

CHRONIC PATTERNS OF REACTIVITY THAT DON'T SUPPORT BOUNDARIES: ENMESHMENT AND DISENGAGEMENT

One way to sort boundaries that aren't serving life is to consider two categories of reactive patterns: enmeshment and disengagement. Enmeshment is a description of a particular set of habits, beliefs, and perceptions that create confusion about who is responsible for what. This pattern often leads to tragic behaviors like blame and demands.

Disengagement is a relational strategy originally used to protect against intrusion and shame. It involves forms of emotional and physical distancing.

Both of these patterns include a reactive relationship to universal needs. Evidence of these patterns indicates a need for healing and long-term support. In the short-term, noticing these patterns and their associated behaviors can alert you to behaviors that are not life-serving and provide the opportunity to interrupt them.

Let's take a deeper look at both of these patterns, beginning with enmeshment.

When you are in enmeshment, you do not have a clear sense of where they end and you begin, and you lose connection with your own center. Enmeshment is like being caught up in a mesh net—hard to separate out one person's experience from another's because they are all caught up together in the same net; personal boundaries are permeable and unclear.

Specifically, it's sometimes hard to know the difference between caring about another's experience and enmeshment. Enmeshment refers to confusion about who is responsible for what. This lack of clear boundaries results in attempts to manage the other person's experience as a substitute for managing your own.

When you think you are trying to contribute to another's well-being, but you are actually acting from enmeshment, there is tension and contraction. This might be as subtle as a forced smile or as obvious as telling the other person to be happy so that you can be happy.

With enmeshment, you notice the other person from a place of vigilance rather than attunement. That is, you watch for any sign of threat. In contrast, with attunement you look for opportunities to receive or offer caring. For example, if your relationship tends toward enmeshment, there's a good chance that you think you know, unconsciously or consciously, the meaning of the

---

ENMESHMENT: PERSONAL BOUNDARIES ARE PERMEABLE AND UNCLEAR

other person's every micro-expression. For every micro-expression that might indicate upset, you perceive it as a threat and you may think to yourself, "I have to fix that." The impulse to manage the other person's emotions immediately follows this thought. You might imagine that you will get a break from managing their experience when they are happy, but from the perspective of enmeshment, if the other person is happy, it's up to you to make sure they stay that way. When your actions fail to manage the other person's experience in the way you want, reactivity in the form of anger, shame, blame, or shut down is usually the result.

From true caring and attunement, on the other hand, you are able to witness another's distress from a place of warm compassion, and so may attempt to offer empathic presence. You have the capacity to be aware of their feelings without losing your center.

Enmeshment is typically not one-sided. Both people in an enmeshed relationship dynamic are likely working hard to manage each other. This is a recipe for losing connection with yourself and building resentment toward the other person.

When you truly want to contribute to another's well-being from the autonomous generosity of your heart, there is attunement and a light expansive feeling. If your attempts to contribute fail, you might feel some sadness or disappointment, but you don't become reactive. You can remain present and connected to yourself and notice what's happening for the other person with care.

From a differentiated sense of caring, you can notice possible upset in another and remain centered in yourself. You have a choice about how you will respond. You can connect with your present needs. You trust and know that the other person is responsible for their own feelings and needs. You trust yourself to set a boundary if they attempt to blame you or make you responsible for their feelings.

Take a look at the table on the next pages, which list the most common signs of enmeshment.

If some of these signs of enmeshment are present in one of your relationships, set the intention to watch for this the next time you are with that person. If you notice a sign of enmeshment, call a pause to connect with your needs.

> WITH DIFFERENTIATION, YOU HAVE THE CAPACITY TO BE AWARE OF THEIR FEELINGS WITHOUT LOSING YOUR CENTER

ENMESHMENT

Enmeshment is a description of a particular set of habits, beliefs, and perceptions regarding relationships. It can be enacted between two or more people when personal boundaries are permeable and unclear. In enmeshment, there is a low tolerance for differences, because they are perceived as a threat. Enmeshment can seem like intimacy to the people caught in this dynamic. Enmeshment is usually a strategy originally used to maintain safety and harmony in the face of violence.

1. You cannot not tell the difference between your own emotions and those of someone close to you.

2. You try to fix, advise, or tell someone what they should and shouldn't do without being asked to do so.

3. When there's a conflict or disagreement in your relationship, you feel anxiety, fear, or a compulsion to fix the problem or convince the other person to agree with you.

4. You imagine you need to rescue someone from their emotions.

5. You imagine you need someone else to rescue you from your own emotions.

6. You and the other person do everything together. It seems like betrayal or abandonment when one of you attempts to do something on your own.

7. You are defined more by the relationship than your own values. You make decisions based on what you think will please the other person.

8. You neglect yourself or other relationships because of a preoccupation or compulsion to be in the enmeshed relationship.

9. Your happiness or contentment relies on your relationship.

10. Your self-esteem is contingent upon this relationship.

11. You take responsibility for meeting the other's needs, even when it is harmful to yourself.

12. You feel the other's feelings. If they feel angry, anxious or depressed, you also feel angry, anxious or depressed.

13. If the other person isn't happy, you think you can't feel happy.

14. You strategize about how to get the other person to feel certain feelings and not other feelings. This might show up as you having a sense that you are "walking on eggshells" or that you "have to" manage the other person's emotional state. For example, you try to cheer them up, explain why they shouldn't feel something, or tell them how to see things differently.

15. You say "yes" and then resent it later.

16. You lose a sense of autonomy when with this person. You find it difficult to express your own preferences clearly.

Disengagement begins as an adaptive strategy to find a sense of stability. By shutting down and shutting out a caregiver who is dangerous or neglectful of your needs, you attempted to create some sense of emotional stability as a child.

But this is not a completely tenable strategy since your survival depends on the ability to cultivate intimacy. As Thomas Lewis talks about in his book, "A General Theory of Love," an infant's life depends on intimacy with a caregiver to regulate basic physiological and emotional functioning. This regulation through connection continues throughout life.

If the reactive pattern of disengagement is present for you, then you had formative experiences in which you moved toward intimacy and got the message that it wasn't okay and possibly that it was dangerous. In your adult life, as you become more intimate with someone, these previous experiences unconsciously motivate you to defend against intimacy.

Defending against intimacy can take a variety of forms. Let's look at three common reactive patterns: mistrust and suspicion, avoidance, and cognitive dissociation.

MISTRUST AND SUSPICION

Disengagement often includes mistrust and suspicion as habits of body, heart, and mind. When there is any ambiguity about what's happening, reactivity sometimes arises to fill in the blanks. The central thinking error with mistrust and suspicion is that if you can predict hurt, it will hurt less when it happens. Thus, your mind can run wild predicting moments of betrayal, rejection, and abandonment. Unfounded mistrust and suspicion can push you towards all sorts of behaviors like spying, encouraging gossip, and asking a lot of investigative questions of the person for whom you have mistrust. Questions like the following are cues that your mind might be caught in this particular form of reactivity:

- Where were you?
- Who were you with?
- Was that person flirting with you?
- Are you really committed to this relationship?
- Why are you late?
- Do you really care about me?

Each time you engage in behaviors like interrogating, seeking gossip, and spying you reinforce the reactive pattern. This reactive pattern blocks the formation of a secure bond which would bring you relief from the anxiety of mistrust and suspicion.

AVOIDING

Avoiding is sometimes a less obvious form of defending against intimacy. Avoidance patterns often leverage socially acceptable behaviors like overworking, becoming intoxicated, and pursuing achievements. If you are running a reactive pattern of avoidance and someone close to you challenges you, you might find yourself responding in one or more of the following ways:

- Denying responsibility with phrases like, "That's just the way I am," or "You're just trying to control me."
- Criticizing the other person and making accusations that they are "needy" or being selfish.

- Gaslighting the other person with phrases like, "You are imagining things." "It's all in your head."
- Making unilateral decisions that affect both of you. This might include, for example, making large purchases with shared money, planning a major trip and telling your friend or partner at the last minute, deciding not to show up at a major event and texting your decision right as it starts.

If you are running an avoidance pattern, you likely resist commitment and opt for vague agreements that leave a way out should intimacy become too much. Even in the moment of making small decisions with someone, revealing what you really want or don't want and committing to an answer can feel scary when you are caught in this pattern. Authenticity seems like a risk. And without authenticity, there is no true intimacy.

Ironically, if you run an avoidance pattern you may pursue a facsimile of intimacy in relationships or situations in which you don't have to fully reveal yourself. Such instances of sudden "intimacy" trigger a rush of pleasant body reactions while not challenging a sense of safety. This can trigger a pattern of addiction to emotionally seducing others.

Of course, all these avoidance patterns block the opportunity to create a secure and healthy relationship to intimacy.

COGNITIVE DISSOCIATION

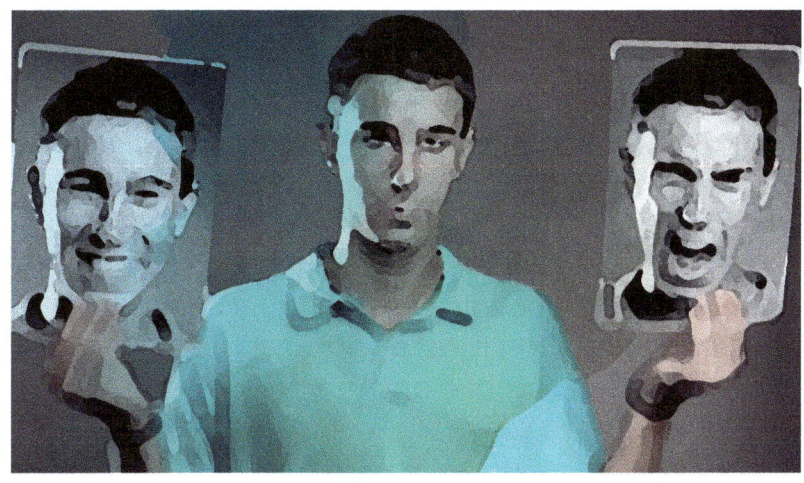

A more colloquial term for cognitive dissociation is compartmentalization. When you hear someone say something like, "I am a different person depending on the situation I am in," they are compartmentalizing parts of themselves relative to role or function. This is different from deciding how to focus your attention. You choose to focus your attention in a certain way at work, for example, but you still maintain a sense of your values, self-connection, and a sense of your life outside of work.

When someone dissociates they lose track of parts of themselves, including their own values. It is this type of dissociation that can lead someone to violate their own or another's values. For example, someone could value monogamy while at home, but while away on business trips they dissociate from this value and have affairs.

Another common example of dissociation is a lack of memory about what was said or done in the heat of an argument such that it is easy for this person to go on as if nothing had happened. In this case, it might seem like the person has recovered quickly, but in reality they have simply compartmentalized the emotion or the difficulty and lost access to their own experience.

For healing, find people who can truly offer consistent authenticity and compassionate presence. Such companionship gives you the opportunity to risk intimacy and experience safety and care.

In sum, relational disengagement is not an expression of independence and autonomy. True autonomy arises from a conscious choice about how to meet needs. In the reactive pattern of disengagement, one is compelled to move away from intimacy. This compulsion is an unconscious relational strategy originally used to protect against intrusion and shame. The behavioral and cognitive strategies* of disengagement are outlined in the following table:

*Conceptualization and Assessment of Disengagement in Romantic Relationships: Robin A. Barry, Erika Lawrence, and Amie Langer

DISCONNECTING/DISENGAGEMENT

Avoidance tactics aimed at minimizing physical contact or communication	Disengagement behaviors that limit or eliminate intimacy	Cognitive Dissociation tactics aimed at perceiving the other person as different or detached from oneself, a loss of shared humanity
You make decisions without considering the impact on the other person and call it independence.	You view intimacy with a sense of mistrust and often suspect that someone may be inauthentic in their expression of care for you.	You share intimate experiences with someone who is an acquaintance, but not with those close to you.
You feel disconnected or indifferent when another person is around.	You lack interest in new activities or pursuing goals. Or, you are overfocused on goals.	You avoid sharing vulnerability and what matters most to you.
You lack curiosity about the experience of others.	You don't initiate contact with friends and loved ones. You often have the impulse to be alone.	As you move towards engagement or closeness, you feel discomfort, anxiety, or you shut down.
You don't care whether others are curious about you.	You often have thoughts of judgment and blame.	You choose to divide up tasks rather than engage in collaboration.

DISCONNECTING/DISENGAGEMENT

Avoidance tactics aimed at minimizing physical contact or communication	**Disengagement** behaviors that limit or eliminate intimacy	**Cognitive Dissociation** tactics aimed at perceiving the other person as different or detached from oneself, a loss of shared humanity
You avoid eye contact.	You minimize feelings. For example: "It's no big deal," "It doesn't matter," "It is what it is," "I am just overreacting," "You're too sensitive."	You criticize and find fault with those close to you; you focus on what you don't like about them.
You will have sex, but don't give and receive affection.	You find yourself spacing out while a loved one is talking to you.	
You don't share about your experience of life, but rather just relate facts or stories about others.	You may feel numb or empty.	

PRACTICE

On this and the following page there is a list of 12 of the most obvious types of behaviors that make it more difficult to maintain Life-Serving Boundaries. Slowly rest your attention on an experience of each one of these. Recall what behaviors, thoughts, body sensations, and feelings come up. For example, if you imagine someone is trying to make you do something, you might feel tension in your chest, lean back, and cross your arms. Once you are clear about what comes up for you when someone is crossing your boundaries, you have cues that can remind you to pause and set a Life-Serving Boundary in such situations.

1. Demanding

2. Persuading

3. Shaming

4. Giving unsolicited advice

5. Guilt tripping

6. Breaking confidentiality

7. Acting from obligation, duty, or guilt when it is not in accord with your values

8. Unwanted physical contact

9. Eye contact that is held too long

10. Sharing personal information that the context or relationship cannot hold

11. Using authority or power to get personal favors

12. Influencing or convincing another to think, believe, or behave in a particular way without asking them if they would be willing to consider a new perspective

Next, use the tables on the following pages to identify cues that a boundary is being violated. Decide which perspective you would like to take—you crossing someone else's boundaries, or your boundaries being crossed—and fill in the table accordingly. The first table has been filled in for you as an example.

EXAMPLE

Your perspective: I perceive someone crossing my boundary by making demands of me

Type of Boundary Crossing: Demands

Body-sensations, posture: Increased heart rate · Shallow breathing · Heat · Throat gets tight · Jaw tightens · Lips pressed together

Thoughts/Words: They have no right to ask that · I could get in trouble if I say no · I should just say yes to get them off my back · I should do what they say

Beliefs: Saying no is dangerous · I am in danger · I have to fight to be seen · I have to fight for my needs

Feelings: Alternately angry and scared · Confused · Hurt · Resentful · Blank/numb

Needs: Respect · To be seen · Safety · Consideration · Mutuality · Fairness · Gentleness · Warmth · Care

Memories/Images: I remember the last time I gave in to a demand from this person · I have an image of this person yelling at me

Energy: Shrinking · Freezing · Drawing in

Behaviors: Stepping back · Looking down · Locking eye contact · Freezing

Impulses: I have an impulse to lash out at them · I have an impulse to run away or hide from this person · I have the impulse to just agree so I can get out of the situation

Your perspective:

Type of Boundary Crossing:

Body-sensations, posture:

Thoughts/Words:

Beliefs:

Feelings:

Needs:

Memories/Images:

Energy:

Behaviors:

Impulses:

SUBTLE BEHAVIORS THAT VIOLATE BOUNDARIES

You could probably list some obvious boundary violations such as nonconsensual touch, name-calling, unsolicited advice, taking what's not given, and sharing confidential information without permission. However, other more subtle behaviors might not register as boundary violations. These can be more difficult to spot in the moment. You might tense up, freeze, or go fuzzy, but you can't quite name what's happening. Becoming more aware of these small moments and finding the words to set a boundary are critical to supporting healthy relating long-term. Let's look at three categories of subtle boundary violations:

1. Lack of mutuality
2. Voice tone and volume
3. Speaking for or about someone

1. LACK OF MUTUALITY

Whether in a professional, familial, or peer relationship, mutuality is a life-serving part of relating. For example, in a professional relationship responsibilities are ideally clear and prescribed. There is mutuality when each person keeps their commitment to these responsibilities. An instance of this might be a medical doctor showing up for your appointment prepared and on time, and you coming with clarity about what you need and how to pay for your visit.

You can reflect on mutuality in a variety of situations. Collaboration is a common one. When you and a peer are working together to make something happen, a lack of mutuality could mean that one person asks the other person to do something differently without examining or offering to change their own behavior. In this example, one person is asked to do more self-reflection and adjusting than the other. When a boundary isn't set within this dynamic, it can escalate into a "power-over/power-under" cycle.

Here are some examples of boundary setting requests with which one could respond in the above situation:

- "I'd prefer for each of us to identify our own behavior with regard to what's working and what could change. Would you be willing to go first?"
- "It will give me a sense that we are on the same team if you could offer to do something different as often as you ask me to do something different. Would you be willing to try this?"
- "I am happy to reflect on what I could do differently; would you be willing to start first with what you want to try?"
- "If something is not working at the moment, could you first offer to do something different or ask me what you could do differently before making a request?"
- "Telling me what I am doing wrong isn't helping. Would you be willing to say what you want instead of what you don't want?"

- "Would you be willing to name what's going well as often as you name what's not working?"
- "This seems one-sided to me. I value mutuality. Would you be willing to identify one thing you could do differently?"
- "Would you be willing to ask for what you want rather than sharing what you don't want?"

An important key to setting Life-Serving Boundaries is to jump in at the smallest bit of discomfort or irritation. The tendency to tolerate small boundary violations or just let things go for the sake of ease or harmony in the moment typically makes it more difficult to set boundaries later. Little boundary violations add up. They can lead you to become ever more reactive and less grounded; then you are likely to have more difficulty accessing the awareness and skill to establish Life-Serving Boundaries.

2. VOICE TONE AND VOLUME

If you read a transcript of a conversation in which tone and volume of voice weren't meeting your needs, the words themselves might seem pleasant enough. Your nervous system, however, responds more strongly to tone and volume than it does to the actual words. When someone is stressed, scared, or caught in judgment, the muscles in their throat constrict and voice volume often increases. While you may have compassion for their experience in the moment, enabling them to engage with you in a reactive way is not a gift of compassion. Instead, it is a message that either you are unaffected by their tone or that it is not important for them to show kindness and consideration to you; either way, you are effectively allowing the behavior to continue.

Here are some possible boundary-setting strategies for this situation:

1. "I want to hear you, but it's difficult with the tone of voice I hear right now. I'm going to take a bathroom break and come back."

2. "The tone and volume of your voice is painful for me to hear. I want to connect and hear you. Would you be willing to soften your tone and lower the volume of your voice?"

3. "Ouch, that tone of voice isn't helping. I'm going for a walk. Let's try again when I get back."

4. "When I can hear your voice from upstairs, my nervous system lights up and I feel stressed. It's so essential for my daily functioning that our home is a sanctuary. Would you be willing to find a way to keep your voice volume lower when you're angry or frustrated?"

5. "I hear you say this is upsetting, and I want to understand what you need. Your tone of voice is painful and distracting for me. Could you pause for three breaths and start again with a different tone of voice?

6. "I won't engage in conversation with yelling." (Walk away.)

7. Talk about tone of voice when it is not happening. Reveal your feelings and needs and set up a simple signal to give when you perceive a tone that distracts you from the connection. This is a helpful strategy when speaking from irritation is habitual for the other person.

8. "I want to have respectful conversations, and this isn't working. Let's try again tomorrow after dinner." (Walk away.)

Again, the longer you wait to set a boundary, the more difficult it becomes. Without clear boundaries a person caught in reactivity will often continue to escalate. Of course, you are not in control of another's reactivity. There is not some right thing you can do to manipulate their behavior or control their reactivity and that is not the goal of this work. When you set a Life-Serving Boundary, you will have the opportunity to observe the other person's response and whether or not they are willing and able to respect your boundaries. You might be pleasantly surprised to see someone rise to the occasion and engage in ways that are life-serving for you both. You might also grieve when you realize someone does not have the capacity to respect your boundaries, and thus choose to end that relationship.

THE LONGER YOU WAIT TO SET A BOUNDARY THE MORE DIFFICULT IT BECOMES

3. SPEAKING FOR OR ABOUT SOMEONE

Speaking for or about someone who is present can be done with the intention to contribute, but more often than not it involves sharing their personal details without permission, misrepresenting them, and excluding them from the interaction.

Sharing even the simplest experiences of someone else without asking is a boundary violation. For example, if you are entering a new group of people with a friend, you might offer a short introduction. But sharing more about them without previous agreement from them deprives that person of the opportunity to build rapport and communicate what is most relevant and authentic for them.

Here are 8 possible boundary-setting strategies for this situation:

1. "Oh, thank you for the introduction, I will jump in here."

2. With humor, "She's talking about me, but I am right here." (Smile and make eye contact.) "Let me finish, I think I know what you were going to say."

3. "Wait, that's about me. I will share stuff about me. Is there something you want to say about your experience of that event?"

4. "You're speaking for me. I would like to speak for myself."

5. "Could you ask me before you share a story that describes my experience and behavior?"

6. "I want to be included. Would you let me answer that?"

7. With excitement, "Oh that's a good story of mine, I would like to tell it."

8. You could also address this boundary violation when it is not happening. Let the other person know the needs that would be nourished if you spoke for yourself. If they say yes to changing their behavior, be aware that willingness does not equal ability. Speaking for others may be a habit for this person. Thus, it's helpful to agree upon a signal or reminder that would be easy for the other person to receive the next time they start to speak for you.

Speaking for someone is often a sign of an enmeshed relationship dynamic. That is, there is a lack of clarity about how to relate with healthy differentiation. Working with a professional or seeking advice from others who seem to access healthy differentiation can help with these kinds of behaviors.

> **LET THE OTHER PERSON KNOW THE NEEDS THAT WOULD BE NOURISHED IF THEY RESPECTED YOUR BOUNDARY**

PRACTICE

Take a few minutes now to brainstorm other common behaviors that are or could become subtle boundary violations. Identify how you have handled these situations with Life-Serving Boundaries or how you might like to in the future.

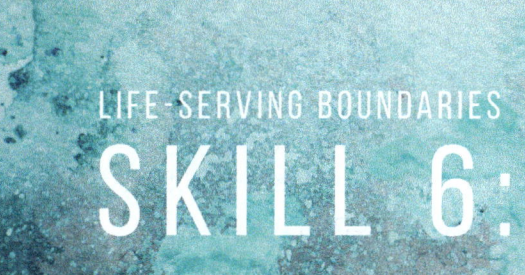

LIFE-SERVING BOUNDARIES
SKILL 6:

ESTABLISH A BOUNDARY WITH BODY LANGUAGE, BEHAVIOR, OR WORDS ANY TIME THAT YOU WOULD LIKE TO CHANGE OR END AN INTERACTION

SETTING BOUNDARIES WITH REACTIVITY

What is reactivity?

Reactivity is defined as the misperception of threat to one or more needs. It can be recognized by at least three main characteristics:

1. A change in physiology, such as heart rate or breathing

2. A stuckness or narrowing of view

3. A loss of access to creativity, skills, broad perspective, wisdom, and compassion

Recognizing reactivity means becoming familiar with the many signs and symptoms that are present. When you fully know reactivity, it can't take over. You get to choose speech and actions that truly serve you and others.

One way to describe reactivity is to reveal the continuum of non-reactive to reactive. It's important to reveal a continuum because reactivity isn't just about the extreme moments. It's much more than that. At the non-reactive end of the continuum, there is responsiveness. You are empty of your own biases, preferences, and agendas for life. You are internally still and open, life flows, and you naturally respond. The most non-reactive moments could be described as unity consciousness, being in the flow of life, or being in the zone.

On the reactive end of the continuum are chronic habits of thinking and unexamined beliefs that lead to seeing the world in ways and making decisions that do not serve life. Fundamentally, reactivity is defined as the misperception of threat to one or more needs. For example, imagine you had a dinner date with someone, but they don't show up where you agreed to meet. You begin to misperceive a threat to needs for care, respect, and consideration. You escalate this sense of threat with thoughts and stories you tell yourself: "People are unreliable. Nobody likes me. I always get stood up. I'm not important. I'm not a priority."

But what if you find out that they did just forget and they don't really want to connect with you? This kind of situation highlights a more subtle difference between reactivity and emotions related to unmet needs. Feeling disappointed and hurt because your needs for consideration and caring aren't met with a particular person is different from telling yourself a story that nobody cares about you or that all people are unreliable. You can feel disappointed about the loss of connection with a particular person without making it mean something about who you are or how the world is. From a non-reactive perspective you remember that you can get your needs met in a variety of ways; and you can feel the grief of needs not being met with a particular person in a particular circumstance rather than creating a story about that.

Boundaries are established in all sorts of ways with body language, behavior, words, and the routines and structures of your daily life. Being able to establish a Life-Serving Boundary at any time means that you have integrated the previous five skills of this Relationship Competency.

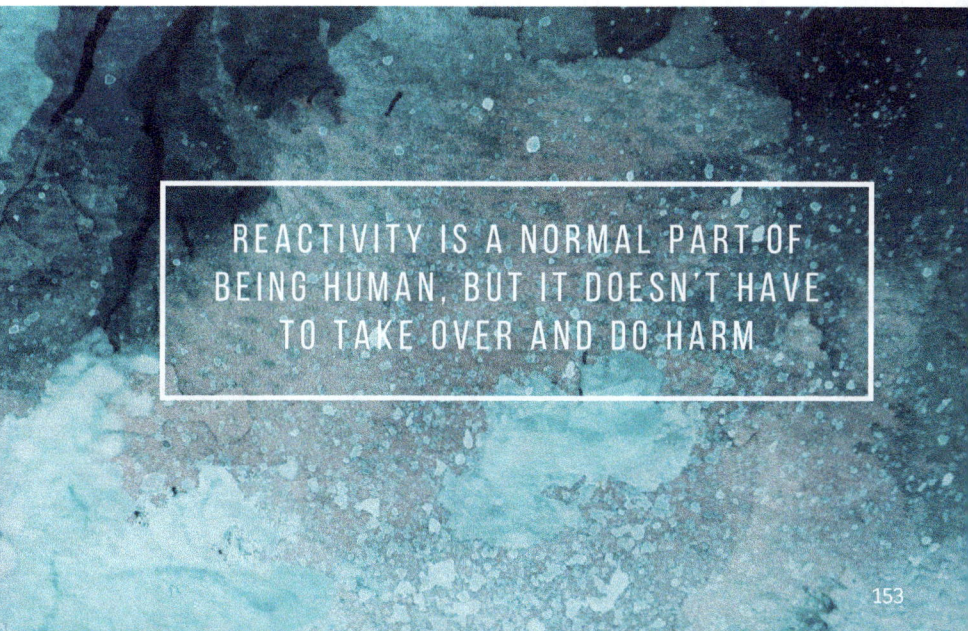

REACTIVITY IS A NORMAL PART OF BEING HUMAN, BUT IT DOESN'T HAVE TO TAKE OVER AND DO HARM

Reactivity is a normal part of being human, but it doesn't have to take over and do harm. As adults, we are responsible for managing reactivity and not letting it splash onto others. When we fail at this, we are responsible for initiating repair. Unfortunately, you have likely not found models for managing reactivity and initiating repair in your family or community. You may imagine that name-calling, blaming, guilt-tripping, or refusing to engage (also known as "stonewalling") are acceptable parts of any relationship. Setting Life-Serving Boundaries with these behaviors is not about expecting someone to be perfect. It's about letting them know that you aren't going to participate in those kinds of relationship dynamics.

Let's look at an example. A Wise Heart student shared that when his girlfriend engaged in name-calling and yelling, he would initially listen and try to defend himself and then he would walk out and call later to try to patch things up. When he called, rather than expressing how her behavior didn't meet needs for him, he attempted to soothe and reassure her and to reconnect.

He didn't wait for her to claim responsibility for her reactivity nor did he ask for repair. In this way, the two of them set a norm in their relationship in which venting reactivity is not only OK, but leads to extra warmth and reassurance later. This kind of repetitive cycle has a high cost and is not sustainable.

Setting a boundary around reactivity means knowing what really helps with handling difficulty and asking for that. In the example above, my student could set a boundary by saying, "What you are saying sounds like judgment to me and I don't want to hear it. I want to hear your feelings, needs, and requests in a lower volume. Please call me when you are willing to do that."

When they talk later, if she is able to express her experience without judgments of him, he might further set a boundary by letting her know that this approach to communication works for him and requesting that when reactivity is present they take a timeout until they can both communicate an internal experience rather than judgments.

Reactive patterns persist when they are allowed to play out. They become well-worn habits. The moment you perceive reactivity in yourself or someone else, release the topic at hand and shift to managing reactivity or setting a boundary.

The most challenging aspect of interrupting your own reactive behavior is that some aspect of you unconsciously believes that expressing yourself in this way will be effective in meeting your needs. Of course, your reactive behavior has been partially effective at one time or another or you would never have developed those habits. It is your greater awareness of the cost of reactive behavior that helps you interrupt reactive patterns and move toward what you truly want.

In the example above, even if this couple successfully has a dialogue that includes repair and boundary setting, they will still fall into the same reactive pattern again before they are able to access a different way of relating. Transformation will occur when at least one of them is able to interrupt the argument earlier, disengage, repair, and recommit to boundaries. Through repeated experiences of successfully interrupting reactivity and engaging new skills, they will build a new norm in their relationship. They will create the new habit of revisiting the fact that a boundary was crossed, acknowledging the cost of that, engaging in repair, and committing to what they need to do differently to support the new way of interacting in the midst of difficulty.

PRACTICE

Take a moment now to reflect on a reactive pattern you have. Write down what it costs you (the negative results of these thoughts, feelings, and behaviors) and what needs this reactive pattern is trying to meet or protect. Write down examples of ways you have met this need when reactivity was not present.

AGREEMENTS AS LIFE-SERVING BOUNDARIES WITH REGARD TO REACTIVITY

Making an agreement is a form of setting Life-Serving Boundaries. Doable agreements about how to handle reactivity when it comes up is one of the skills involved in setting boundaries. Making agreements around reactivity requires that you accept that the same reactivity will occur again. Accepting this, you then have at least two tasks.

First, it's essential to become intimately familiar with reactive patterns. You want to get to know them like you know your closest friends. With a close friend you can recognize them from a distance. You know their shape, how they walk, what they wear, etc. When you know reactivity this well you can quickly spot it, even when it is just barely appearing in the background, just as you would recognize your friend at a distance.

To recognize reactivity earlier, take time to reflect on moments in which it comes up for you. Name all the little signs that lead up to it. Identify all dimensions of your experience: thoughts, energy, posture, behavior, physiology, impulses, feelings, needs, and beliefs. Also, take note of the circumstances preceding your reaction such as lack of sleep or food, pressure from a work deadline, a stressful time of day for the family, etc. The more you know about your reactivity the more you can anticipate it arising, and the more quickly you can intervene with yourself.

The second aspect of making doable agreements regarding reactivity is to shift your focus from what you won't do to what you will do. Make an agreement with yourself and the other person about what you will do at the first sign of reactivity. It doesn't matter if the reactivity is in you or the other person. You don't have to point out who is getting reactive. In fact, telling someone else they are reactive usually makes things worse. Small doable behavioral responses to reactivity often include things like:

- Take three deep breaths before speaking
- Ask for a time-out, say "I'm reacting, could you say that in another way?"
- Decide on a nonverbal signal to stop action—like putting your hand on your heart, going for a walk, repeating a mantra, etc.
- Engage in a regulation strategy that is right for you. You can find a list of regulation strategies in the appendix.

If you have an agreement about how you will meet reactivity and can keep that agreement, the occurrence of reactivity can be trust building rather than trust eroding.

SETTING BOUNDARIES WITH REACTIVE EXPRESSIONS OF ANGER

When a friend begins to express anger by expressing judgments of someone else, you likely feel torn. On the one hand, you know that under anger your friend is feeling some version of hurt, fear, or sadness, and so you want to offer support. On the other hand, your own integrity and care for others comes up when you hear harsh judgments. You don't want your friend to misconstrue your willingness to listen as agreement with their judgments about other people.

Discerning how to set a boundary in a connected way starts with self-connection. Ask yourself, "Do I have the resources to be a grounded empathic listener, or am I already starting to feel reactivity?" Let the other person know which is true. For example:

"I have the space to hear you and offer empathy."
OR
"I notice I am not really able to be present right now."

It's useful to make the distinction that you are offering to listen with empathy and not just volunteering to be a receptacle for someone's venting. Venting is a form of reactivity. It's not helpful and has a negative impact on the listener. In contrast, asking if someone is willing to hear you express yourself freely with the intention to connect, can demonstrate self-responsibility. When you know the other person has the intention to connect, you can trust the process and be patient while hearing judgements and complaints.

Keep in mind that it is not the feeling of anger itself that necessarily presents a challenge, but rather whether or not the other person lets anger escalate and express itself in ways that trigger disconnect and division. Even after you agree to listen, you can set boundaries regarding that listening.

SET BOUNDARIES WITH LISTENING

"What's important to you in this?"

"I can't stay present for those kinds of judgments of others, but I do want to hear what you want in this situation."

"It's painful for me to hear those judgments of the other person because I value compassion. Would you be willing to tell me about your experience or what you want to change in the situation?"

"I'm getting overwhelmed, I need to take a break."

If you are not able to set boundaries, then you will likely begin to argue with your friend. You might say things like:

"Oh come on, they aren't all bad."

"They are just human and make mistakes."

"You are blowing this out of proportion."

"Just try to see their side for a minute."

Trying to talk someone out of their judgments or pushing them to have empathy for the other person before connecting with their own feelings and needs often escalates reactivity. If you are not able to hear the other person's judgments as a tragic expression of feelings and needs, then it is a good time for you to set a boundary or simply exit the conversation.

Someone caught in escalating anger might attempt to get you to agree with their perspective of the situation. This strategy is called collusion. It is a tragic strategy that is attempting to meet needs for support, acceptance, or empathy. In fact, collusion is not a demonstration of empathy, but merely a demonstration of adding more reactivity.

In the case of being pressured to agree, it's important to stand in your own integrity and honesty. Perhaps it might sound something like this:

STANDING UP TO PRESSURE

"Your experience is valid whether I agree with your perspective or not."

"I'm happy to share my take on things once you really have a sense of being heard, but while you are still angry, I don't think sharing my take will be helpful."

"I wasn't there and I don't know the whole situation, so it doesn't make sense for me to form an opinion."

"I don't find agreeing or disagreeing very helpful. What I'm interested in is your needs and how to support you."

"I'd rather focus on supporting you and getting your needs met."

"I care about you and I am willing to offer empathy."

"Is there another way I can show you that I care about you and support you other than agreeing?"

It's true that sometimes people get very attached to meeting their needs through getting agreement. In the little and big picture, the idea that having a caring connection means we have to agree all the time has led to incredible violence and suffering. When you stand in your integrity and find another way to connect, you are doing something much more significant than just attending to that one interaction. You are supporting a consciousness in which differences are no longer a threat, but a cause for curiosity and celebration.

PRACTICE

Take a moment now to reflect on the last time someone expressed judgments to you of another. What was your first impulse: to move away, to calm them down, to argue, to set a boundary, or to offer empathy?

What would have supported you in staying connected with yourself in that moment?

REACTIVITY AND BOUNDARIES IN NEW RELATIONSHIPS

In new relationships, setting clear boundaries is one of the fastest ways to know whether the relationship has potential to work long term. If your dating partner, new friend, or new coworker can't or won't respect your boundaries now, it could be a long, slow, painful learning curve ahead. Spare yourself this pain and set boundaries early and often in your new relationships.

It can be difficult at the beginning of a relationship to be direct and clear about what works for you and what doesn't. Your own chronic reactive habits might push you to avoid conflict at all costs.

For an example, let's look at the context of a new dating relationship. You really like your new dating partner. You've been going out for three months now and you are starting to hope this could really work. Then, on your next date they are two hours late. They arrive and explain how band practice went late and that they lost track of time. You feel disoriented. You're not sure what's happening, but you know you don't want to threaten the sweet connection you have enjoyed so far. So you decide to just be understanding and say it's okay and that you understand how that happens sometimes.

Shockingly, the same thing happens on your next date, but this time there is a different explanation and an apology. You are not hiding your disappointment so much this time and maybe you even say a word or two about what it was like for you to wait two hours. You receive more words of apology, and within the hour you are happily receiving the love and affection for which you had been waiting.

If this pattern continues, it often escalates in a predictable way. You complain more each time the other person is late. Complaining escalates into anger and criticism. You find yourself taking potshots at the other person at random times. Your dating partner at first intensifies the apology, possibly even crying. But later, the apology gets equal time with justification and, at the worst moments, there are attempts to belittle or dismiss your feelings and needs. If the belittling goes on too long, you might begin to doubt yourself or try to control them.

This is a very painful way to learn about the results of not setting clear boundaries at the beginning of a relationship. Let's go back to our example and consider the first time this dating partner is two hours late for your date and see how boundary setting might look. There you are standing in front of your attractive, but very late date. You are a swirl of confusion, hurt, disappointment, fear, and desire. Your date is explaining the lateness and trying to reassure you that it doesn't mean anything. You are in an emotional pressure-cooker; you need time to find a sense of groundedness before responding. So the first thing you do is buy yourself some time. For example, you might say, "I don't know what to say right now. Let's get something to eat and talk about it after."

Once your emotions and body have settled and you have done something grounding with your date like eating or walking, you will be able to sort things out a bit. From a grounded place you realize that a number of things can be true at the same time and you can express them freely.

In this particular example, you can name at least three things that are true:

- You feel disappointed and hurt this evening because being two hours late doesn't give you the sense of respect and caring you're looking for.
- You know that you really like this person and have enjoyed your time together thus far.
- Trust and reliability are important for you in any relationship and arriving two hours late doesn't contribute to either. If being late is a pattern for this person, it's not going to work for you.

As you express these things, perhaps one of the most important things is that you value this truth and honor yourself as you speak. If you express your truths with an apologetic tone, your dating partner will likely interpret that you don't really mean what you say or it's not important.

Another key element in expressing this is to follow up with a connection request to see if the message sent was the message received. A connection request is one that asks another to connect with what was just said or say it back. It could sound like this: "I really want to make sure I am speaking clearly. Would you be willing to tell me what you understand about what I said?"

Next make an action request and really hear the answer. A clear request might sound something like this: "Would you be willing to prioritize being on time for our dates and to call me if you will be arriving later than ten minutes after the time we agreed to?

After making a request, it is important to hear the real answer. Your dating partner might respond like this:

"Oh yeah, I will. You are important to me. It's just that I get caught up in things and I lose track of time. You know I really value being in the flow. Once I get creative, I want to follow that creative energy. Art isn't created on a schedule you know."

In this case your dating partner starts with yes, but then really implies a no. If you let this roll by without further negotiation, you might drop into the reactive pattern described above. It's hard to stay with it, because moments like these can be deal breakers. When the immediate pain of a potential breakup is looming, it's hard to keep track of the long-term satisfaction that comes from clearly expressing what's right for you and sticking to it.

So, don't be hard on yourself if in the moment you can't stay clear and continue the negotiation. If you feel yourself get fuzzy, just name that: "I get fuzzy hearing you say that. I'd like to talk more about this later when my head clears."

In summary, here are key elements that can support you in setting boundaries early and often in a relationship:

- When the other person does something that crosses a boundary, delay talking about it until you can get grounded. This might be a few minutes or a few days.

- From a grounded place, name what's important to you in that situation. These things might include:

    - Your feelings and needs at the time of the boundary crossing

    - Your care for the other person

    - A clear articulation of your boundary along with a specific doable request

- Don't settle for a "maybe" or "I'll try" as a response to your requests. You can follow up with: "Can you think of anything that might get in the way of your being on time or letting me know if you will be late?" Continue the negotiation until you either come up with a new request that works for both of you or you hear a clear yes or no to your initial request.

SETTING BOUNDARIES WITH REACTIVITY AND LETTING GO OF RESOLUTION

Wanting to get out of the discomfort of not having resolution can push you towards boundary violation. Have you ever followed your partner around the house trying to resolve something after they called a time-out, or vice versa? Setting boundaries often means being willing to tolerate the discomfort of disconnect and unresolved conflict.

A popular bit of advice that I hear couples quote is, "Don't go to bed angry." I cringe when I hear it because I know the price they often pay when they follow this: hours and hours of yelling, blaming, and judging. It's much better to go to bed angry than to reinforce these reactive habits. You can acknowledge your anger and your desire to resolve it the next day and perhaps set a time for talking.

When you are attached to getting resolution with someone, you are not only likely to reinforce reactivity, you might also let the other person cross boundaries that you hold just fine with everyone else. You know you wouldn't hang around while a store clerk blamed you for the hard day they were having by saying something like, "It's your fault I got so upset. You had too many groceries!"

However, when someone close to you says something like, "I wouldn't be so upset if you hadn't criticized me!" you get hooked. You want to be seen. You want the other person to see that your intention was to make a request, not to criticize. You want to be connected and you want fairness. Naturally, you make an attempt to clarify another's misperception. Too often your attempts to clarify are perceived as a denial of their experience. The other person then escalates; voice volume increases and you experience words and actions that don't meet your needs for kindness and respect. When you remain in a dialogue after your boundaries have been crossed, you inadvertently send a message that it is okay to cross your boundaries. Your willingness to continue the interaction under these conditions is the same as saying, "I am willing to give up my need for respect in order to be close to you." This is a recipe for continued reactivity and violence.

When reactive patterns like this have been established over a long period of time in a relationship, letting go of immediate resolution is a critical part of the change process. Your ability to tolerate the discomfort of being disconnected from someone you normally enjoy connection with allows you to set boundaries around behaviors that do not meet your needs. It also allows you to interrupt reactive patterns rather than practice them. Here are three keys to strengthening your ability to tolerate disconnection and let go of pursuing immediate resolution:

KEYS TO LETTING GO OF IMMEDIATE RESOLUTION

1. Build trust in your skills for self-empathy, self-soothing, and seeking support from friends and family.

2. Cultivate a critical mass of clarity by reflecting on the cost of staying in an interaction when your boundaries have been crossed.

3. You can find ways to articulate your boundaries by knowing the needs they are designed to meet. For example, a person being "yelled at" might say, "I need respect and peace and so I won't continue this interaction until your voice volume lowers." Or, "This way of interacting doesn't have the caring I am looking for. I am going to do something else now. I hope we can connect tomorrow."

PRACTICE

Take some time now to reflect on one time recently when you set a clear boundary in an interaction and one time when your attachment to resolution led to boundaries being crossed. Where do the three keys listed above fit into both situations?

UNDERSTANDING THE DIFFERENCE BETWEEN LIFE-SERVING BOUNDARIES AND THREATS

As you move forward making agreements around reactivity, it's important to understand the difference between making a threat and setting a boundary. Two key distinctions involve intention and honest expression. Let's look at these distinctions with an example from a couple, Gustav and Inez.

Last night Gustav got drunk and communicated in some ways that didn't meet Inez's needs for respect and caring. Inez could find no way to connect with Gustav in his drunken state. The next day, she decided that if this happens again, she will take care of herself by leaving the house and spending the night with her sister. She expressed this decision to Gustav. Hearing this, Gustav accused her of threatening him.

Gustav might think Inez is threatening him because he assumes her intention is to hurt or punish him. This is because he recognizes that Inez has made a decision to behave a certain way based on his actions. A behavior-dependent response is commonly associated with intent to punish, but also occurs without any intent to punish. For example, if Gustav began visiting his brother on Friday nights, Inez might say something like, "If you are going to visit your brother on Friday, I am going to go out with Susan." This has the same element of behavior-dependent response, but would likely not be heard as punishment or a threat.

Gustav might also hear a threat because Inez arrived at her plan to leave the house and spend the night elsewhere on her own and not in collaboration with Gustav. Not hearing Inez's honest expression, it is easier for Gustav to interpret her decision as the punishment of being shut out.

So how can Gustav and Inez avoid this merry-go-round of misunderstanding and pain?

Gustav can take responsibility for his interpretations by offering the honest expression of stating them aloud and asking for clarity:

"When I hear your decision to stay at your sister's the next time I drink, I imagine you are trying to punish me. I need clarity. Is this your intention with this decision?" This opens the opportunity for Inez to clarify with honest expression:

"Gustav, last night when you were drunk and talking

to me in the way you did, I was feeling scared and hurt. I needed safety and respect. So, I am wanting to take care of myself better the next time you are as intoxicated as you were last night. Leaving and spending the night at my sister's is a strategy for self-care."

Essentially, a threat implies the intention to harm with the hope of changing someone's behavior. Setting a Life-Serving Boundary clarifies both what needs are important and what the limits are for a particular negotiation.

When either person has clarity about the intention to protect a particular need, a collaborative dialogue might open up about how they can repair what happened and do something differently in the future.

However, in some cases, negotiations have been made again and again around a particular behavior and there has been no change. At this point, one partner may simply reach a tolerance limit. For example, let's say that Inez and Gustav work out ways to handle the situation, but perhaps they have been unable to implement their solutions or those solutions have not effectively addressed their pain. Inez may then set a boundary by unilaterally choosing to take care of herself; she may leave the house or find another strategy to address her needs. This kind of decision-making can meet needs for structure and clarity in the relationship and provide a clear message about what is not workable in the relationship.

As you sort out the distinctions between making a threat and setting a Life-Serving Boundary, ask yourself the following questions:

- What needs am I trying to meet or protect with the Life-Serving Boundary I am setting?
- Does any part of me have the intention to punish or get even with the other person? If yes, can I engage in self-empathy for this part or ask for empathy from someone else?
- Is needs-based negotiation with the other person possible? What would give me a sense of safety and predictability if I engage in such negotiation?

QUESTIONS FOR REFLECTION

Where in your relationships do you tolerate something that you imagine could change?

Choose a particular relationship and situation that seems most approachable to you for transforming.

Are you willing to express observations, feelings, needs, or requests to initiate a conversation about a change with that person?

HOW TO REPAIR BOUNDARY VIOLATIONS

Relationship repair is Relationship Competency 10 in Mindful Compassionate Dialogue. When you learn the skills of relationship repair, you can remain centered in times of disconnect. You trust that you can find your way back to connection in the face of hurt and anger. Relationship repair builds confidence that your relationships can weather the most difficult of times.

Relationship repair means coming back together after an experience of disconnect and unmet needs. It includes any action, internal or external, that rebuilds connection. Repair requires the intention to connect and take responsibility for your behavior by naming what didn't work, offering empathy, and making a plan to do something differently next time.

Relationship repair is most effective when you take care of reactivity before you begin a repair dialogue. Self-empathy and empathy from someone outside of the conflict will help prevent blame, shame, and defensiveness, which are common in a repair dialogue. By dissolving reactivity in specific ways before you initiate repair, you will be able to maintain focus on connection, empathy, and honesty. Repair can then become an opportunity to build trust and to learn how to move forward in new ways.

Repair dialogue differs from other dialogues in that it specifically addresses interactions or behaviors that trigger disconnect. A feeling of disconnect is often accompanied by other feelings like anger, guilt, shame, depression, or shut down. When such difficult feelings are present, you might engage in tragic strategies for repair such as blame, arguing over the details, or building a case to prove that you are right.

In Mindful Compassionate Dialogue self-empathy and a desire to reconnect are the first steps in a repair dialogue. Connection and shared vulnerability are the path towards healing, care, and building trust.

With the intention to connect, instead of asking who did what wrong and assigning blame, you ask questions to help you connect with yourself and the other person before engaging in a repair dialogue. Using the feelings and needs list (included in the appendix), ask yourself these questions:

SELF-REFLECTION BEFORE REPAIR DIALOGUE

1. Which of the "four alarms" feelings are present for me? (See below for a description of the four alarms).

2. What other feelings are present for me? What feelings do I guess are present for the other person?

3. What needs are present for me now, both met and unmet? What needs do I guess are present for the other person, both met and unmet?

4. What needs was I trying to meet when I behaved in a way that led to disconnect? What needs do I guess the other person was trying to meet when they behaved in a way that led to disconnect?

5. Assuming we will be in a similar situation in the future, what might support me in making a different choice? What could I do in the present that will help bring about a different experience in the future? What do I request of the other person to do differently next time?

THE FOUR ALARMS

Guilt

Guilt means you are telling yourself you should or shouldn't have **behaved** in a certain way.

Guilt arises when your **behavior** seems to be or is out of alignment with a value/need of yours. Guilt is often accompanied by thoughts of duty, obligation, and what you should or shouldn't be doing. For example, "I should have gone with my partner to see their folks." Guilt, like all feelings, lives along a continuum of intensity. Here is an example, with intensity increasing from left to right:

Sorry — Contrite — Remorseful — Culpable — Guilty

Shame

Shame means you are telling yourself you should or shouldn't **be** a certain way.

Shame arises in regard to your **identity**. It arises when you think that you are not being the person you think you should be or would like to be. Behind shame there are thoughts (often unconscious) that are some version of, "I have been a bad person and deserve punishment." Taking action out of shame can land you into the violent concept of repentance in which someone else decides how bad you are and doles out a punishment. Shame is often just outside of conscious awareness and so can be hard to identify. Shame also often stimulates a state of shut down making it difficult to do any self-reflection or reach out for support. Out of shame, you may unconsciously stop asking for what you need and just go along with whatever your partner says. Shame, like all feelings, lives along a continuum of intensity. Here is an example, with intensity increasing from left to right:

Self-Conscious — Embarrassed — Disgusted — Shame

THE FOUR ALARMS

Shut Down or Depression

Shut down means you are telling yourself that you should or shouldn't **experience** a certain feeling, impulse, dream, etc.

Shut down arises in regard to your **experience**. It is a signal that you are denying or pushing away experience, including feelings and needs, as they arise in you. You may have some thoughts that you don't deserve to have your needs met or that there are certain feelings and needs you shouldn't have. You may have had training from family, school, and community that gave you the message to deny your own needs in favor of pleasing others or being "strong." Shut down, like all feelings, lives along a continuum of intensity. Here is an example, with intensity increasing from left to right:

Uncomfortable — Cranky — Conflicted — Disconnected — Listless — Bored — Numb — Shut Down — Depressed

Anger/Blame/Defensiveness

Anger/blame means you are telling yourself that others should or shouldn't **be or behave** in a certain way.

Anger arises in regard to **others or external events**. Behind anger there are thoughts that things should be different than they are or someone should behave differently. The word should can lead you quickly to a disconnected state. In the context of recovering from a relationship where your needs were not met, anger can also indicate progress. Anger can be an important indicator that you are beginning to recognize that your needs have been unmet and it is good to stand up for your needs. However, if action is taken from anger, violence and unmet needs will result. Anger, like all feelings, lives along a continuum of intensity. Here is an example, with intensity increasing from left to right:

Discomfort — Discontent — Resistant — Grumpy — Impatient — Irritated — Annoyed — Frustrated — Defensive — Angry — Furious — Irate — Enraged — Livid

The willingness to give and receive empathy is the next important part of repair. When you are struggling with difficult feelings, it's helpful to remember that offering empathy does NOT mean condoning, agreeing with, or liking the behavior of the other person. It means attuning to the feelings and needs of the person. When you are disconnected, empathy may sound robotic or stiff at first. Typically, several rounds of expressing and reflecting back feelings and needs is required before a sense of connection returns. Using the feelings and needs list is essential in this step to prevent a slip into shame or blame. It's important to go slow while expressing your feelings and needs and offering empathy. You can find a table outlining the repair process in the appendix. When you offer empathy and then quickly shift to your own experience, empathy doesn't have time to land and repair is difficult to establish.

Ineffective models of repair are often associated with admitting you're wrong and asking for forgiveness. Labeling something "right" or "wrong" doesn't inform new actions. It's important to express regret for behavior that didn't meet needs for another and genuine care for the impact on them. This doesn't mean shaming yourself or trying to punish the other for their actions. Effective accountability requires connection, understanding the needs that went unmet, and a commitment to do something different in a future similar situation. This means identifying and negotiating specific doable actions and requests to make new agreements.

Lastly, it's helpful to remember that repair isn't instantaneous. It occurs little by little as connection is built and trust is earned through new behaviors. The discomfort of the rupture in connection may lead to immediate relief through repeating expressions of pain and anger and demanding multiple apologies. When you and the other person can be present with the pain and discomfort without going back to the story of the event, empathy can sink in and healing can begin.

Effective relationship repair requires mindfulness, self-awareness, and subtle skills. When these are present, repair can happen relatively easily. As you gain trust in your ability to repair ruptures in connection, you may still experience them as painful but will also see them as opportunities for deepening your understanding of yourself and the other person. They can grow your capacity to love.

As you attempt a repair dialogue, watch for the following common ways that repair gets derailed:

4 COMMON WAYS REPAIR GETS DERAILED

1. **Insecurity:** To the extent that you are unsure about the validity of your own feelings and needs, you will tend to shame, blame, analyze, minimize, dismiss, criticize, defend, use "shoulds,"

and compare. You may need empathy from someone outside of the situation in order to accept your own feelings and needs.

2. **Reactivity:** Holding onto your story of who someone is based on past events to such a degree that you cannot take in new information in the present is a form of reactivity. This often means you will perceive a threat when none is present. If this is happening, you may need outside support to help create a greater sense of safety in the interaction.

3. **Fear of Disharmony:** When fear of disharmony is informing your decisions, you likely don't trust that repair is possible. You might then ignore interactions that don't meet your needs. When you ignore your needs, resentment grows.

4. **Lack of Skill:** When there is a lack of skill regarding self empathy, empathy, and honest expression, you may have good intentions, but don't know how to create repair without falling into the old model of blame and shame. It's essential to invest in learning and practicing new skills.

REPAIRING BOUNDARY VIOLATIONS

Repair in the context of boundary violations is the process of building trust that the boundary will be respected in the future.

As you begin repairing a boundary violation it's helpful to consider some assumptions you might be holding about what's required for repair. Some people assume that repair has to happen with the person who violated your boundary. However, when a boundary violation has been severe, it may be important to end contact with that person to protect safety or wellbeing. Boundary repair is still needed whether you are in contact with that person or not.

If you do want to start a repair process with the person who violated your boundary, the first thing you are likely looking for is an apology. Unfortunately, apologies are often associated with shame, defensiveness, justification and no real connection or repair. Apologies also often involve assigning blame and offering forgiveness in the sense of returning someone's "goodness" to them. This kind of apology lands you in painful power dynamics rather than repair. What you really want is to know the other person understands the impact of their actions on you and feels regret and care about that. You also want to know that this will translate into taking responsibility and behaving differently in the future.

> WHEN A BOUNDARY VIOLATION HAS BEEN SEVERE, IT MAY BE IMPORTANT TO END CONTACT WITH THAT PERSON TO PROTECT SAFETY OR WELLBEING

Still, you like to hear people say they are sorry. Sorry is a common strategy for receiving care. Naturally, you want to know that the other person cares about you and therefore cares about whether your needs were met or not by their action. You also hope that if they say sorry they will avoid that same behavior in the future. Unfortunately, when someone offers an apology out of guilt, shame, or defensiveness, the likelihood that they will understand better how to respect your boundaries in the future is pretty low. The more likely outcome is avoidance and a quiet harboring of guilt or resentment.

Repairing a boundary violation requires much more than an apology. It requires mindful dialogue based on empathy and honesty, a commitment to behave differently, and an opportunity to earn trust through engaging in a new way. A mindful dialogue for repair has a very different tone and approach depending on the type of boundary you want to maintain in that relationship. In general, for distant boundaries you share less of your inner experience and focus more on your specific and doable request.

Let's look at the steps for repair in a situation in which someone violates your boundary, as well as an example of you attempting repair after violating someone else's boundary. I will also give examples of dialogue with three different boundary types: close, flexible, and distant.

6 STEPS TO TAKE WHEN SOMEONE VIOLATES YOUR BOUNDARY

1. Identify the specific behavior(s) that was experienced as a boundary violation.

2. Identify the feelings that came up for you when that occurred (fear, confusion, shock, frustration, discouragement, disappointment, anger, etc). If this is a close relationship, express these directly. If this is a more distant relationship, name these for yourself and/or receive empathy from someone outside the situation.

3. Identify the needs that were not met for you. Most likely it will be one or more of these: respect, consideration, honor, safety, clarity, or comfort.

4. When you have had sufficient empathy for yourself, identify or guess at the needs that the person who violated your boundary was trying to meet when they behaved in the way they did.

5. Create an agreement about what will be done differently in future interactions in a similar context. Or, if you are not going to interact with that person, make a decision about what you will do in future similar situations that will support you in maintaining your boundaries.

6. If you continue interacting with the other person, mindfully observe over time if the agreement is kept and if it is contributing to repair and building trust.

When engaging in repair regarding boundaries, you are likely choosing one of the three options in the table below.

CLOSE BOUNDARY
Establish a shared memory or at least understanding of the example you wish to talk about. "Do you remember when we were (describe time and place) and you (describe behavior in observational terms or offer quote if it was a verbal violation)? That didn't work for me. When I think about that I feel _____. I am looking for more _____ (needs). Can you tell me what you heard? Once you are heard, ask what feelings and needs were alive for them when they engaged in the behavior that crossed a boundary. In the future, would you be willing to _____ (make a request for what behavior you would like to experience in a future similar situation, not just 'don't do that again')?"

FLEXIBLE BOUNDARY
Make a connecting request: "I would like to share something that's come up for me. Are you available to connect?" Follow the steps above, offering the level of vulnerability that you trust this person can hold regarding the given situation.

DISTANT BOUNDARY
Share your decision about what you will do to take care of your needs in a future similar situation or simply decide this without sharing it. If you do share, it might follow this simple structure: "Next time, I will take care of myself by_____ (specific and doable request for yourself)."

6 STEPS TO TAKE WHEN YOU HAVE VIOLATED SOMEONE'S BOUNDARY

1. Identify the specific behavior(s) that was experienced as a boundary violation.

2. Guess the feelings that were up for the other person when you violated their boundary either aloud with them or in your own heart depending on the vulnerability and type of boundary in that relationship.

3. Guess the needs that were not met for the other person when you crossed their boundary, either aloud with them or in your own heart depending on the boundary in that relationship. Or, ask if they would like to share what didn't work for them about your behavior. The most common unmet needs with a boundary violation are: respect, consideration, honor, safety, clarity, and comfort.

4. Identify the needs you were trying to meet when you violated the other person's boundary. Share this or not depending on what supports connection.

5. Create an agreement or make a decision about what will be done differently in future interactions in a similar context.

6. Check in with the other person over time to ask if this agreement is contributing to repair and building trust.

BASIC CONVERSATIONAL STRUCTURE AFTER VIOLATING SOMEONE'S BOUNDARY

1. "Do you remember when (describe time and place and your behavior)? I am guessing you were feeling _____ and that wasn't the sense of _____(need) you wanted. Is that right?"

2. Listen to the other and reflect back the experience you hear them describe. Offer empathy.

3. "Hearing how that was for you, I feel regret and sadness because I care about you and I want to respect your boundaries."

4. "Next time I commit to (your new behavior). OR Do you have an idea about what I could do in the future that would work better for you?"

   (If they answer with, "Just don't do that again." you can agree and create even more safety and repair by coming up with something you WILL do that will meet the needs of both of you.)

CONCLUSION

To maintain Life-Serving Boundaries as a conscious practice, it will be important to have support and reminders. I recommend you engage with Wise Heart classes, either live or self-paced. I have also provided a summary of each skill below that I recommend you either copy and post somewhere that you can review it frequently, or rewrite it in your own words.

SKILLS REVIEW

SKILL 1

The first skill is, when saying "no" to someone's request, identify the needs to which you are saying "yes." Whenever you prioritize or determine things that are important to you, you are inevitably saying no to other things. You just need to determine what needs and values you are protecting when you say "no."

SKILL 2

The second skill is to identify the three types of useful boundaries. There are distant boundaries, flexible boundaries, and close boundaries.

In order to determine where a relationship might fall between these three types of boundaries, we can evaluate the supportive context or conditions of the relationship, your needs and intention or expectations, the body language typical of the relationship, what and how much you are willing to share with that person, and whether or not it is a peer relationship.

SKILL 3

The third skill is to articulate three non-negotiable boundaries that you hold in any relationship. You do this by determining things that you are not willing to do or engage in, as well as things that are top priorities for you and cannot be negotiated away. Again, it is helpful to recognize the needs that are being met—the needs you are saying "yes" to—when you set these boundaries.

SKILL 4

The fourth skill is to identify current limiting beliefs that interfere with boundary setting, and the expansive beliefs that will support boundary setting. For example, a limiting belief might sound like, "If I want to be in this relationship or group, I can't be myself. I have to be a certain type of person to belong." On the contrary, an expansive belief might sound something like, "I can be authentic and be accepted."

SKILL 5

The fifth skill is to identify the signs and symptoms of behavior in yourself or others that don't support boundaries. This includes paying close attention to bodily cues of tension, anger, or fear as well as specific words or behaviors commonly associated with boundary violations. When you become aware that someone is crossing your boundaries, you can utilize a pause-action phrase to give yourself time to regroup and respond with a request for yourself or the other person.

SKILL 6

The sixth and final skill is to establish a Life-Serving Boundary with body language, behavior, or words any time that you would like to change or disengage from an interaction. Again, this might start with a pause-action phrase like, "Give me a minute." It will then likely include a specific request—either a request for the person you are speaking to, or a statement about your own action.

Setting Life-Serving Boundaries is about being firmly grounded in self-respect and getting clear about what truly helps you thrive in your life. From the framework of Mindful Compassionate Dialogue, a Life-Serving Boundary means making a conscious decision about how you will relate to another or behave in a particular situation. These decisions depend on clarity about what meets needs and what doesn't, relative to what others do and share and what you do and share. Such clarity allows you to put your attention and energy where you want it to go by consciously adjusting what and how much you share with others.

As with all 12 Relationship Competencies in Mindful Compassionate Dialogue, becoming competent and confident with Life-Serving Boundaries requires mindfulness, compassion, integration of the consciousness of connection, attention to healing, conceptual understanding, and skills practice.

With deep gratitude for your dedication to transformation and growth, I send you a wish for a thriving life!

Radiating love from my heart to yours.

—Elia Paz

APPENDIX

Empathy: "Do you feel _____ because you need (what's important to you is, you value,...) _____?"

Honesty: "When I (see, hear, or notice) _____, I feel _____ because I need (because what's important to me is, because I value) _____.
Would you be willing to _____?"

Feelings

Happy
Joyful
Elated

Grateful
Appreciative
Touched
Moved
Expansive

Eager
Giddy
Excited
Thrilled

Pleased
Content
Satisfied
Fulfilled

Curious
Interested
Absorbed

Healthy
Alive
Vigorous

Relieved
At ease
Mellow
Rested
Relaxed

Friendly
Affectionate
Loving
Passionate

Energetic
Adventurous
Exhilarated

Clear headed
Alert
Focused

Calm
Peaceful
Serene
Tranquil

Safe
Comfortable
Secure
Confident
Empowered

Hopeful
Heartened
Inspired

Worried
Apprehensive
Scared
Panicky
Terrified

Restless
Nervous
Anxious
Dread

Cranky
Tense
Agitated
Stressed
Overwhelmed

Lonely
Vulnerable
Hurt
Heartbroken
Anguish
Agony

Dejected
Despondent
Depressed

Disconnected
Detached
Bored

Tired
Exhausted
Burnt Out

Impatient
Irritated
Frustrated
Exasperated
Resentful
Defensive
Angry
Furious

Disappointed
Discouraged
Disheartened

Concerned
Alarmed
Shocked
Disturbed
Appalled
Horrified

Sad
Teary
Tender
Grief stricken

Regretful
Sullen
Downhearted
Hopeless
Despair

Confused
Disoriented
Torn
Ambivalent

Jealous
Envious
Bitter

Embarrassed
Guilty
Shame

Empathy: "Do you feel_____ because you need (what's important to you is, you value,...)_____?"

Honesty: "When I (see, hear, or notice)_____, I feel_____ because I need (because what's important to me is, because I value)_____.
Would you be willing to_____?"

Universal Needs / Values

Empathy	**Security**	**Purpose**	**Honesty**
Intimacy	**Predictability**	**Meaning**	**Integrity**
Connection	**Consistency**	**Competence**	**Authenticity**
Affection	**Stability**	**Contribution**	**Wholeness**
Warmth	**Trust**	**Efficiency**	**Fairness/Equity**
Love	**Reassurance**	**Growth**	**Expression**
Understanding	**Reliability**	**Learning**	**Creativity**
Acceptance		**Challenge**	
Caring	**Partnership**	**Discovery**	**Peace**
Bonding	**Family**	**Inspiration**	**Groundedness**
Compassion	**Presence**		**Hope**
Communion	**Mutuality**	**Order**	**Healing**
Spirituality	**Friendship**	**Structure**	**Harmony**
Sexuality	**Companionship**	**Clarity**	**Ease/Comfort**
Kindness	**Support**	**Focus**	**Completion**
Gentleness	**Collaboration**	**Information**	
	Consideration		**Nurturing**
Autonomy	**Seen/Heard**	**Appreciation**	**Food/Water**
Agency	**Acknowledgment**	**Celebration**	**Rest/Sleep**
Choice	**Belonging**	**Mourning**	**Safety**
Freedom	**Community**	**Aliveness**	**Health**
Spontaneity	**Inclusion**	**Humor**	**Shelter**
Independence	**Participation**	**Beauty**	**Movement**
Respect		**Play**	**Touch**
Honor		**Joy**	

SELF-REGULATION STRATEGIES

BODY

Soften: Soften your face, mouth, jaw, tongue, shoulders, back

Orient: Orient to one of the five senses: sounds, light, color, scents, taste something or touch something that has a soothing texture

Self-soothing touch: Put your hand on your heart, give yourself a shoulder massage, run your hand through your hair, rub your thighs, rub your feet back and forth on the floor, etc.

HEART

Wishes for well-being : Express a wish for the well-being of yourself or others: May I feel peace. May she feel love. etc.

Sing: Sing a soothing song silently or aloud

Love: Bring to your awareness to someone you love easily and feel your love for them

MIND

Visualize: Visualize something that immediately brings a sense of peace and calm

Name: Name parts of experience: thoughts, feelings, needs, impulses, etc.

Chant: Repeat a mantra or meaningful phrase

ENERGY

Expand: Imagine your energy extending out beyond your body

Direct: Direct energy through the soles of your feet into the earth. Visualize and sense this flow of energy

Attend: Attend to the cycle of energy that flows from your crown down through your centerline to your root and back up

A RELATIONSHIP REPAIR PROCESS

After beginning with self-empathy (which includes checking in with the four alarms), the following parts could be done in any order. The most important thing is to make sure all parts reach completion before starting another part. If you jump quickly from one thing to another, it is usually more difficult to get to repair. Remember, you can only repair one instance of unmet needs at a time. When you try to address years of unmet needs in a single dialogue, it is very difficult to get repair.

SELF-EMPATHY

Engage your anchor. Separate what actually happened (observation) from your interpretations and judgments.

Name the needs you thought you would meet at the time you decided to do what you did. Really connect with the energy of these needs you held and your good heart in attempting to meet them. AND/OR Name the needs that were unmet by the other person's behavior. Take time to mourn the unmet needs. Feeling your own grief can help with creating acceptance of the situation rather than continued judgment or blame.

EMPATHY

Offer empathy for the impact of your behavior on the other person	**Ask for empathy regarding the impact of another's behavior on you**
"When you remember me saying or doing ___, do you feel ___, because your needs for___ weren't met? Is that right? Did I miss anything?"	"What would help most is to be heard with empathy. Would you be willing to say back the feelings and needs I expressed?"

HONEST EXPRESSION

Respond to the pain in the other person

"When I hear you are hurting, I feel regret. I am sorry and disappointed because I care about you and your needs. I will do something different next time. Can you tell me what you are hearing me say?"

Share the feelings and needs alive for you when you think about the behavior of the other person that didn't work for you.

"When I think about what you did, I feel ___ because ___ (need) is so important to me. Can you tell me what you heard me say?"

ACTION REQUESTS

Together, brainstorm what new actions you will take in consideration of both the other person's needs and your needs in a future similar situation.

- The process of brainstorming action requests begins when you feel connected and heard.
- Action requests are the beginning of a negotiation.
- Action requests are concrete and do-able. As such, they include a specific time, place, and action.
- Action requests may be a baby step on the path to new behavior.

ABOUT THE AUTHOR

ELIA PAZ

I am enormously grateful to the very many teachers and mentors I have had along the way, and the enormous work others have done over many decades that have served our understanding of what it means to heal and live a fulfilling life.

Ever since I can remember I have devoted myself to this search for living life from love and wisdom. As a young adult this led to a bachelor's degree in psychology and a graduate degree in school psychology.

In 2001 I found Compassionate/Nonviolent Communication (NVC) and began training with Marshall Rosenberg and other internationally known NVC trainers. I immediately knew that

Compassionate Communication was the missing piece. For me Compassionate Communication is the hands and feet of spirituality. In 2006, I was certified as a NVC trainer.

In 2002 I spent a year living in Great Vow Zen Monastery. Here I was able to do much healing work and deeply integrate NVC into my internal dialogue. Now the inner voice of compassion arises as habitually as the old voices of self-criticism and judgment did in the past.

I founded the English portion of Wise Heart in 2007. (Our Spanish site was established in 2021).

At about the same time I entered into three years of training in various mindful experiential approaches to therapy such as: Hakomi (body centered therapy), attachment theory, trauma treatment modalities, Recreation of the Self, Matrix group process, and character theory. Shortly thereafter, I completed introductory training modules in Emotionally Focused Therapy and with the Gottman Institute.

In 2015, I—together with the support of my colleagues—created a comprehensive system of transformation and thriving relationships called Mindful Compassionate Dialogue.

In 2020, Wise Heart became established in Spanish through collaboration with many, including my current business partner, Fer Matteo, in Argentina and team leader in Bolivia, Violaine Felten-Arredondo.

Today I enjoy a thriving life filled with friends, family, animals and nature. I rejuvenate and find play in gardening, caring for the land and animals, doing art, and movement.

www.ingramcontent.com/pod-product-compliance
Lightning Source LLC
Chambersburg PA
CBHW070741160426
43192CB00009B/1533